BR
115
.C5
B78a
1949
v.2

THE LIBRARY OF THE
MENNONITE BRETHREN BIBLE COLLEGE
77 KELVIN ST., WINNIPEG 5

Call No. **901**
Author No. *B.897.ch*(II).
Date *Nov./1959.*
Acc. No. *7824*

CANADIAN MENNONITE UNIVERSITY
LIBRARY
500 SHAFTESBURY BLVD
WINNIPEG, MANITOBA
CANADA R3P 2N2

CHRISTIANITY
AND
CIVILISATION

II

PRESS OPINIONS ON PART I

" A masterly philosophical survey of the problems of ontology and truth "—*Observer*.

" It is impossible to exaggerate the interest and value of these Lectures "—*Manchester Guardian*.

" Marked by lucidity and ease of exposition . . . One of the most distinguished Continental theologians of our time "—*Spectator*.

" For one reader at any rate, this is ' the book of the year ' "—*Holborn Review*.

CHRISTIANITY AND CIVILISATION

By
EMIL BRUNNER

SECOND PART:
SPECIFIC PROBLEMS

GIFFORD LECTURES DELIVERED AT
THE UNIVERSITY OF ST. ANDREWS
1948

LONDON: NISBET & CO., LTD.
22 BERNERS STREET, W.1

First published in 1949
Reprinted 1955

MADE AND PRINTED IN GREAT BRITAIN

PREFACE

THIS second series of my Gifford Lectures, given at St. Andrews University in March 1948, is complementary to the first. While the first was an attempt to work out something like a Christian philosophy of civilisation dealing with some basic principles which underlie all civilisation, it is the scope of this second series to give a Christian interpretation of some of the main features of civilised life. Many readers may miss some other aspects, such as marriage and the family, which they feel of equal if not of greater importance than those treated in this book. If so, I completely agree with them, but having been compelled to restrict myself to nine such subjects (in the tenth lecture I attempt to give a synoptic view of the whole field), I think it justifiable to leave out some of the topics which have been in the focus of Christian thought throughout the ages as well as in recent times.

As a matter of fact, I am not so much afraid of the reproach of having treated too few, but rather of the criticism of those who think I have tried to deal with too many subjects. I hear them ask how any one man can claim to have competent knowledge of so many different sectors of civilisation, each being almost infinite in itself. Again I fully share this view. There is probably no one—at any rate not the author—who can make such a claim. Still, it so happens that my life is concerned with all of these sectors and I have to try to lead it as a Christian, and the same is true of thousands of my contemporaries. While it is necessary that Christian men and women particularly competent in one of these fields should speak and write about the relation of the Christian faith to that particular matter, it seems to me legitimate, and even necessary, that alongside these monographs of specialists someone should at least try to give a synoptic view of the whole (even if he has no expert knowledge of a majority of these subjects), provided that he has given to all of them prolonged thought as a Christian.

Perhaps I would not have dared to form such a plan had I not, in lecturing about one of those subjects which is particularly remote from my own experience—that of technics, or should I say technology?—received much encouragement from groups of experts, both professors and practical technicians. None the less, I am sure that in every one of these lectures there is much to be criticised by those who do have expert knowledge in that particular field. They may be assured that they will find me sincerely grateful for their criticisms; indeed I have been so conscious of the inadequacy of my knowledge and my lack of experience that on several occasions I have felt like giving up altogether.

This view of my task made it imperative not to try to give my lectures an apparent weight of scholarship by quoting many books. The only scholarship to which I might lay claim is that of a theologian or Christian thinker, who has made up his mind to apply some of the basic Christian doctrines to some of the problems of civilisation or culture, of which the urgency is felt by every live Christian.

The brevity of these lectures, compared with those of most of my predecessors, is mainly due to the fact that for reasons of language I could not afford to prepare two sets of lectures, one for fifty minutes' delivery, the other for publication. Even within this limitation I should not have succeeded had I not received most generous help from colleagues at St. Andrews, particularly Professor Donald Baillie and Professor W. R. Forrester. Again I wish to thank many other good friends, both within and outside St. Mary's College, for their sympathy and hospitality, which made my stay in their town a happy experience which I shall not forget.

E. B.

CONTENTS

PREFACE v

I. TECHNICS 1
   Technics as old as man. The problem of technics new, resulting from the technical revolution. Technical man precedes technical revolution. Robinson Crusoe. Effects of the technical revolution on man. The tragic coincidence : technical revolution in the age of secularisation. Means and ends reversed. The spiritual cause of this reversal. The fatal course of technics—towards the abyss ? Ethical appeal and education inadequate. The Christian alternative to the technical apocalypse.

II. SCIENCE 16
   Science younger than technics. Its relation to truth. Natural science and *Geisteswissenschaften*. The scientific ethos. Its Christian basis. No necessary conflict with faith. The influence of sin upon science. Scientific mythology. Science and the postulate of " religious neutrality ". The value of Christian anthropology for the *Geisteswissenschaften*. Science within the totality of human destiny.

III. TRADITION AND RENEWAL 29
   The modern age anti-traditional. Tradition : cultural memory. Christianity and tradition. Christianity guardian of Greek cultural values. Social tradition and social rootlessness. Christianity and change. " Not yet " and " no more ". The newness of life in the Gospel. The revolutionary force of Christian faith. Renewal of centre and periphery. Revolutionary conservatism.

IV. EDUCATION 43
   Education and community. The Socratic programme of education. Its incomparable influence. Its relation to Christianity. The German idealist idea of *Bildung*. Its aristocratic character. The original Christian idea of education. Its deformation by theological intellectualism. The Reformation ignores the Socratic element. Pestalozzi's rediscovery. Kierkegaard's contribution. Secularist education in our age. The Christian idea in the modern setting.

CONTENTS

V. WORK 57

Why do men work? The classical (Aristotelian) conception of work. Its influence in the middle ages. The Marxist idea its counterpart. Luther's rediscovery of vocation. The modern crisis of the "motifs" of work. Its essential causes. Collectivism unable to restore the dignity of work. The Christian conception of work, both as stimulus and as moderating force.

VI. ART 72

Comprehensive conception of "art". The mystery of art deeper than beauty. Imaginary elevation of existence. The danger of aestheticism. The second commandment. "Christian art"? Form primary in art, but art presupposes human depth. Art in relation to Roman Catholic and Protestant religion. Can art survive secularism? The metaphysical basis of passion. Formalism and barbarism. Art and "the sabbath".

VII. WEALTH 86

Material presuppositions of cultural life. Personality and property. The abstract material good, money and credit. Its danger for personality and community. Capitalism according to Marx. Wealth in the light of the Bible. No Biblical system of economics. Ethical interest in economic structure. Communism necessarily totalitarian. The dilemma of social security and the free society. Christianity and the economic motif. Onesidedness of Max Weber's theory concerning Calvinistic capitalism. Christianity and secularist materialism.

VIII. SOCIAL CUSTOM (*SITTE*) AND LAW . 101

Destruction of social habit by individualistic rationalism. Social habit basis of personal morality. The New Testament and social habit. Along with artistic "style" social habit destroyed in the last century. Law filling the gap. Natural and positive law. Positivism. Pre-state and state-Law. Gospel and Law. The created order. Equal rights in Stoicism and Christianity. Polarity of personal rights and social obligation. Law and sin. Secularism increases coercive law.

IX. POWER 114

Restrictive definition. Having and using power. Will-to-power. Material and spiritual elements in power. Power and freedom. Limiting and monopolising ultimate power, the state. The " division of power ". State sovereignty and God-sovereignty. The unlimited state power, the totalitarian state. Power in inter-state relations. The attempts to limit national sovereignty. The universal world state in the light of Christian faith. Culture, power and religion.

X. THE CHRISTIAN IDEA OF CIVILISATION AND CULTURE 127

Coming back to the first lecture. What can Christian civilisation mean ? Man alone produces civilisation. Essence of civilisation. Its basic motifs. Civilisation human, but not *the* Human. Why it is " formal ". The place of civilisation and culture in the Christian conception of life. Some objections answered. The Christian idea : the human above the cultural ; the physical-spiritual unity of man ; the civic element fundamental, therefore civilisation above culture. The place of tradition and education. The " highest cultural values "—how far ? Art and science in the service of God and of man. The present chances for the realisation of the Christian idea.

EPILOGUE. CHRISTIANITY BEYOND CIVILISATION 140

CHRISTIANITY AND CIVILISATION

Second Part: Specific Problems

I

TECHNICS [1]

AMONGST all the problems of civilisation with which we are dealing in these lectures, the problem of "technics" is the youngest. All the others have worried Western mankind and Christianity for centuries; not so technics. In earlier times people had hardly become conscious of it, much less did they think of it as a problem. To-day, however, it is in the front line, because—to a degree previously unheard of—technics—or shall I say technology?—determines the life of man, endangers the human character of civilisation, and even threatens the very existence of mankind. Whilst half a century ago the startling progress of technology was the basis of an optimistic philosophy of life and progress, since the two world wars, and particularly since the first atomic bomb was dropped on Hiroshima, the conception of technics has become more and more connected with gloomy, even desperate, perspectives for the future. The question whether civilisation and mankind will survive has become *the* problem of the hour, so that we cannot but start with it.

This fact—that technology has recently become the most urgent of all problems—contrasts strangely with the other fact that technics is as old as humanity. Human history begins with the invention of the first stone tool, that is, with technics. It is in the shape of *homo faber* that man first shows himself as a being transcending nature. From this beginning technics, that

[1] Part of the material of this lecture has been used in an article of *The Christian News Letter*, 1948.

is, the creation and use of artificial tools serving the life of man, has increasingly distinguished man's life from that of the animal, and imprinted upon it a specifically human character. The history of technics from its beginning to, say, the time of James Watt, is characterised by an almost unbroken, more or less equable and, therefore, quite unobtrusive progress. Step by step man makes headway in solving the task which he recognises as his own, to subdue nature by his technical inventions.

We distinguish the first epochs of human history by their technical character, speaking of the stone age, the bronze age and the iron age, where an almost unnoticeable transition from one to the other makes the distinction difficult. The same is true of what we call historical man, as we find him first in the Delta of the Nile, in Mesopotamia, in the great valleys of China and of India, where the history of civilisation has its origin. Everywhere the development of technics is the hardly perceptible and therefore often forgotten basis of political, social and cultural change. Nowhere does this technical evolution assume a revolutionary aspect, never does it appear as a break with the past. All epochs and all nations in history are equally technical and therefore none is so in an outstanding sense. That is true also of Western history as it first appears as a characteristic unity in the Roman Empire; it is true of the Middle Ages and up to the beginning of the 18th century; but at that moment it is as if this underground current suddenly broke through the surface. The curve of development which hitherto had been a continuously and almost imperceptibly rising straight line, abruptly takes the form of a parabola becoming steeper and steeper. Technology begins to become a great revolutionary power and within the last few decades it has taken the lead in the life of the Western nations, and even of the whole world. It has become the dominating factor of modern civilisation. The changes which technology has wrought in the last two centuries are beyond all comparison with those in previous ages. That is why our epoch is called the age of technics, and why the problem of technology, unknown to previous epochs, has suddenly become the most urgent problem of all.

Why is this so? We *might* answer this question first by pointing to the tempo of technical inventions and the changes created by them. The mad speed of technical progress makes mankind breathless; with one invention pressing fast on another, man cannot get any rest. The growth of technics is out of proportion to the progress made in other departments of life, and puts to shame all attempts of society to adapt itself to the technical change in order to make it useful and beneficent. It is like what happens when a youth suddenly begins to grow at a great pace. His spiritual development cannot keep pace with his bodily growth and therefore there are disturbances.

TECHNICAL EVOLUTION

YEARS OF HISTORY 4000 3000 2000 1000 1 1000 1800

There is a disproportion between bodily and spiritual growth, the one taking place at the cost of the other. This comparison, with its emphasis on the time-aspect of technical evolution, is certainly legitimate. It is true that technical evolution and change acquired such a speed that the balance of power within society was disturbed and that the social changes, which would have been necessary to adapt life to them, could not be made adequately. We might say that the mushroom growth of giant cities, with their apparent poverty of structure and their production of a mass-society and mass-psychology, was a kind of surprise-effect produced by lack of time for adaptation. In a similar way, one can attribute the preponderance of technical interest in our generation to this speedy development of technics.

But such an analysis remains wholly on the surface. More than that: it falsifies the picture of real history by making the cause the effect and the effect the cause. This idea of social adaptation lagging behind technical progress rather hides than reveals the truth. It is not technics which has created the modern man, but it is the modern man who has created technics. The technical man existed before technics. Take as an example the most famous novel hero of the age immediately preceding the technical revolution, Robinson Crusoe. Compare Robinson Crusoe with his colleague in suffering, Ulysses. How differently they face their identical lot of being cast by shipwreck on a solitary island! There is not much difference, technically, between Robinson Crusoe and Odysseus. Perhaps the most important difference is that Defoe's hero, in distinction from Homer's, has and uses gunpowder. But the main difference is this, and this is exactly what Defoe wants to show: how Crusoe masters technically his hopeless condition. This is the inspiring idea which has made the book a favourite of youth: the idea of the man who helps himself out of the difficulties, the man who—ingenious in quite another sense than Ulysses—is capable of subduing hostile nature step by step.

Behind the technical evolution of the last two hundred years there is a much deeper spiritual process, with which the first part of these lectures has dealt. This process begins with the Renaissance, leading on to the Enlightenment, and beyond it to the radically positivist secularised man of to-day. Modern technics is the product of the man who wants to redeem himself by rising above nature, who wants to gather life into his hand, who wants to owe his existence to nobody but himself, who wants to create a world after his own image, an artificial world which is entirely his creation. Behind the terrifying, crazy tempo of technical evolution, there is all the insatiability of secularised man who, not believing in God or eternal life, wants to snatch as much of this world within his lifetime as he can. Modern technics is, to put it crudely, the expression of the world-voracity of modern man, and the tempo of its development is the expression of his inward unrest, the disquiet of the man who is destined for God's eternity, but has himself rejected this destiny. The hypertrophy of technical interest, resulting in a hyperdynamism of technical evolution, is the necessary consequence of man's abandonment to the world of things, which follows his emancipation from God.

Let us return for a moment to those quiet periods which nobody would call technical, though even then technics had reached a high measure of development and was incessantly progressive. What do we mean by "technics"? In the first place, domination over nature, emancipation from its hazards by intensifying and multiplying the functions of bodily organs. The hammer and the crane are the fortified fist and the prolonged arm, the car is the improved foot, and so on. The whole of technics is a continuation of what nature has given to man as his particular character: upright walk. That is why technics is, as such, a task given to man by the Creator, that Creator who gave man the upright spine and thereby the freedom of the use of his hands and the eye directed to infinitude. God wants man to use his intelligence in order to rise above nature and "*subdue the earth*". This phrase is found on the first page of the Bible. It immediately follows that other phrase in which the specific nature and destiny of man is expressed: "*and God created man in His own image*". It is not by chance that the second precedes the first. The task of subduing the earth follows from the the first. The task of subduing the earth follows from the nature and the destiny given to man by the Creator. It is most likely that the author of this first chapter of Genesis was thinking of the upright walk of man, but this physical presupposition of his superiority is the expression of a deeper reason for superiority. Man is called to transcend nature, because he is called to be godlike. Technics is only one of the forms of nature-transcendence, but it is that which presupposes the others, higher civilisation and spiritual life.

So long as man does not use artificial means, he remains dependent on what nature gives, here and now. That is, he necessarily remains on a low, more or less animal, level of development. He is completely at the mercy of natural hazard and tied to the moment; he cannot look into the future, he cannot shape his life, he must live it as nature gives it. By the invention of artificial tools, man emancipates himself to a certain degree from the dictates of nature. The technics of housebuilding and agriculture make him independent of what nature gives at each particular time and place. With a roof over his head and four walls around him, he can defy the weather and live where he chooses. By agriculture he dictates to the earth what to produce for him and to produce it in such a measure that he can store up enough for the future. He makes water or wind drive his mill. He captures the wind in his sail and forces it to carry him over the seas. The spinning-wheel and the loom make him independent of the scarce animal-skins for clothing. One by one he cuts the thousand ties by which his body and its needs are linked to the fortuitous formation and production of the ground. The development of crafts of all sorts leads to differentiation of human society and to the specialised training and development of spiritual capacities; it leads to exchange, to the communal life of the city, to communication between town and town, between country and country. The crafts are at the same time a preparation for higher arts and, in the form of artistic trade, they play their part in aesthetic ennoblement.

Technical skill can be learned and, therefore, transmitted from generation to generation. That is why in this sphere of life there is an unambiguous and more or less continuous progress. Each generation learns from the one before and adds new inventions. In this process of technical education the mind is trained for methodical work. The multiplicity of crafts makes for a rich differentiation of the spirit. It cannot be denied that cities, with their differentiated crafts, are pre-eminently the seats and nurseries of higher culture and education. All these organic types of technics—if I may so call them—are easily forgotten in our age of highly abstract mechanical and therefore inhuman technics. But they belong to the true picture and show the close relation between technics and truly human civilisation.

Even in this picture of pre-modern technics, however, there

are traits of a more sinister quality. Closely related to the tool, and often expressed by the same word, is the weapon. The development of crafts almost everywhere gives rise to the development of war technics. There are exceptions to this rule, one of the most interesting being that of the older China, where an almost unique development of crafts did not lead to a parallel development of war technics, because war and fighting were stigmatised, culturally and morally. Not even the invention of gunpowder, which in Europe had such pernicious consequences, could become dangerous among this peaceful people. The moral discredit of war was so deep that gunpowder was never allowed to be used for war purposes, and its dangerous energy was puffed out in harmless fire-works. But apart from this most honourable exception, the development of technics generally resulted in increasingly dangerous weapons and wars. The Roman technics of roadbuilding was developed primarily for military purposes. The technics of shipbuilding created the navy, and so on. Still, all this remained within limits which prevented technics from being the dominating potential of war.

Another danger to society resulting from technical development is the formation of social classes. Technical, like military, superiority creates differences of property, social privilege and power. These differences, however, so far as they were conditioned by technics, did not become very dangerous in the pre-modern ages, because it was not so difficult to acquire technical skill and technical means. From all this, we can conclude that on the whole the positive, beneficial aspects of technical progress by far outweighed the negative or evil ones. In the "golden age of the crafts" nobody would have thought of technics as a serious danger or even a problem of civilisation.

All this is suddenly changed with the introduction of machine technics. It had a sort of prelude in the invention of gunpowder and its application to warfare. The consequences of this invention were far-reaching and could give a premonition of what further similar leaps in the development might mean. It is strange and somehow shameful that Christian Europe did not succeed in doing—perhaps did not even attempt to do—what had been achieved by the Chinese. At any rate, with gunpowder, technics begins to acquire a negative trait in European history. But incomparably more revolutionary was the invention of the steam engine and the locomotive, and later on the discovery and technical use of electricity and of petrol, the invention of light metals and the development of chemistry. Now begins the technical age. As we said before, we should not look upon these inventions as the real causes of the technical revolution; they had to come, because men wanted them. They had to develop at such an unparalleled rate, because men did not want to limit their development in any way. Still, once technics had become what it is now, its effects upon the social and spiritual life of mankind are tremendous.

It has often been said, and it is obviously true, that all the technical changes which took place in the life of men from the stone age to James Watt are not nearly as great as those since James Watt. The life of a farmer or craftsman before the invention of the steam engine was not so different from that of Jeremiah's time as from that under modern agriculture and industry. Machine industry in the broadest sense of the word, including transport and communication, has changed not only the life of Europe and America, but that of the whole surface of the world, in a tempo and in a measure completely unparalleled before.

This technical revolution has its positive as well as its negative side. By it man has indeed subdued the earth in a measure inconceivable before. By the radio he has eliminated distance completely, so far as mental communication is concerned; by the aeroplane he has eliminated it almost completely, so far as bodily communication is concerned. The techniques of production are capable of nourishing, clothing, housing every inhabitant of this earth in more than sufficient degree and with almost complete certainty. Hunger and want are no more inevitable. That they are still amongst us is entirely conditioned by political, social, international power-relations, preventing the reasonable use of technical possibilities. Medical and hygienic techniques would be sufficient to create everywhere conditions of life which would guarantee to a high degree a healthy life and development of the child and double the average age of man. The invention of cinema and radio, perfecting that of the printing-press, allows an almost unlimited spreading of cultural assets. In a measure then, present day technics places at the disposal of man the means which would safeguard a high standard of life and give access to cultural advantages to everyone capable of understanding and valuing them. Technical mankind has a superabundance of all things needed, and a superabundance of means to transport them wherever they are needed. If there were no war, if there were only just and reasonable laws, if all men were well-intentioned, technics would provide, so it seems, almost a paradise. The technicians can claim that it is not their fault if, at this hour more than ever before, mankind presents features of the utmost misery and the most unworthy conditions. All this is meant by the phrase " technical progress ", which up to recent years was used without hesitation. It seems as if technics—and particularly modern technics—was an indisputable gain for mankind.

Why is it, then, that nobody at this hour uses that word " progress " without hesitation, if at all? Let us be clear that there is no such thing as " technics in itself ". The production of a cannon is a technical affair, but at the same time it is the expression of a certain political and military will. The production of dangerous narcotics is a matter of chemical industry, but it serves purposes which are medically and morally unsound and pernicious. Technics, therefore, is never purely technical. It always stands in the closest connection with the totality of social and cultural life and of man himself. " Technics " is an abstraction which does not exist. There are only men working technically for certain purposes. When modern man conceived the idea of redeeming himself and making himself master of his life by technics, he did not know or divine that such technics would have results of a very different order. What, then, are those effects of the technical revolution which an increasing majority of modern men abhor?

Modern technics does not mean merely a fantastic extension

of man's power over nature: it also means millions of men working underground, uncounted millions of men massed together in soulless giant cities; a proletariat without connection with nature, without a native heath or neighbourhood; it means asphalt-culture, uniformity and standardisation. It means men whom the machine has relieved from thinking and willing, who in their turn have to "serve the machine" at a prescribed tempo and in a stereotyped manner. It means unbearable noise and rush, unemployment and insecurity of life, the concentration of productive power, wealth and prestige in a few hands or their monopolisation by state bureaucracy. It means the destruction of noble crafts with their standards of quality and their patriarchal working conditions; it means the transformation of the farmer into a specialised technician of agriculture, the rise of an office proletariat with infinitely monotonous work. It means also the speedy standardisation of all national cultures and the extinction of their historical originality. It means universal cliché-culture, the same films and musical hits from New York to Tokio, from Cape Town to Stockholm, the same illustrated magazines all over the world, the same menus, the same dance-tunes. It means the increasing domination of quantity over quality, not only in production itself but also in the formation of social, political and international power.

Above all, there are two phenomena in very recent times which, like devilish monsters, rise from that progressively technified mankind: the modern totalitarian state and modern technical war industry. It cannot be said that the totalitarian state is the necessary product of technics, but its relation to technics is obvious. Without modern technics the totalitarian state is impossible. And the tendency towards totalitarianism lies within technical evolution: mechanisation, centralisation, mass-men. Modern war industry, however, is the direct product of modern technics. Let us remember it is not the technicians that are guilty, but man who has abandoned technics to itself, incapable of bridling its development, putting technics without hesitation, and, as if driven by necessity, at the service of his political power-aims. This war machinery displayed its terrifying force in the first world war. The second world war manifested its increased destructive force; but since then there has come that last step or leap: the use of atomic energy, which means a sudden increase in the capacity of annihilation without analogy in the previous history of technics. Now the development of technical warfare has reached the point where nothing is impossible to it. Mankind for the first time faces possible universal suicide.

This is the other, the dark side of the picture. It shows how dangerous it is to speak of technics *in abstracto*. One could have known from the history of technics that every technical advance does not change merely man's relation to nature, but also man's relation to man. Every invention is an increase in power, and every increase in power within society is a danger to its balance and order. This fact could remain unnoticed so long as technical progress could be assimilated socially and ethically. It is the tragic fact of modern history that the technical revolution took place at a time when mankind was in a process of social dissolution and ethical confusion. It was the era of progressive secularisation and mass-atheism, when all ethical standards were relativised and men became metaphysically and ethically homeless. Cause and effect mutually interpenetrate each other. We have already seen that modern technics could not have developed without a certain spirit of rationalism and secularisation. It is, however, equally true that secularised humanity was not socially and ethically equal to the technical revolution. Only a society which was incapable of subordinating the profit motive to higher motives, a society which was ethically, and even aesthetically callous and enfeebled, could allow the growth of those soulless, ugly, giant cities, with their speculative building and their proletarian quarters. Only such a society could watch without protest the dissolution of all natural community, and accept as inevitable the development of modern war technics.

In this connection we have to point out grave fault on the part of the Christian Church. The Church ought to have been on the watch-tower. She ought to have seen what was going on behind those beautiful slogans of freedom and progress. The Church might have been expected to protect men from enslavement and from becoming automatons. The Church ought to have seen that in such conditions, which upset all the order of creation, the preaching of the Gospel became almost illusory. Is it not shameful for the Christian society that Confucian China was capable of suppressing the military use of gunpowder, while the Christian Church could not prevent, and did not even try to prevent, the development of a war machinery incomparably more dreadful?

European industrial history is not altogether devoid of indications of what might have happened if modern industry had developed within a truly Christian society. I am thinking of a certain phase in the industrial development of Great Britain and Switzerland. Within a few decades of the invention of the steam engine these countries experienced a physical and social devastation within the working population which was definitely alarming. But then moral and religious forces reacted and were called to the defence. By social legislation, by the trade-union and co-operative movements, and by something like an awakening of social consciousness through prophetic personalities, much of the damage was repaired in a comparatively short time. What had been called technical necessity proved quite unnecessary. The technique of fabrication, so often regarded as being beyond ethical control, was effectively put under such control. Many things remained bad enough, but yet the effect of this ethical-social reaction against the technical materialistic *laissez-faire* gives us a faint idea of what could have been avoided if society had awakened in time to the ethical dangers of so-called progress.

Nobody can say how far the disease of uncontrolled, unassimilated technics has progressed already, whether the disease has reached the point where it becomes incurable or not. It is our duty, however, to open our eyes to the imminent threat to life and to do whatever we can to make technics serve human ends.

The nature of technics is to place at man's disposal the means for certain purposes. Of course, the production and use of technical means is in itself a purpose, but it is never a *Selbst-*

zweck, an ultimate purpose. It is essential to the health of a society that this order of ends and means should be known and recognised, so that technics as the sum of means is subordinated to man's life. Where the means become more important than the end, where technics becomes autonomous, a social disease develops, which is analogous to cancer: autonomous growths, not useful but injurious to the organism, which develop independently of the organic centre and finally destroy the organism. When, for instance, a country rejoices over the growth of a city of millions of inhabitants, this is as stupid as if someone were to rejoice over the growth of a cancer. Giant cities are merely symptoms, but they are obvious symptoms of autonomous technical growth which finally leads to destruction.

The positive meaning of a human civilisation depends on this subordination of means to ends. The reversal of this order, therefore, results in civilisation becoming inhuman and finally perverted. For this reversal of the order of ends and means, which produces a demonic autonomy of technics, secularisation is more to blame than technics. It is because the world and its goods become to men more important than God, eternal life and love, that men throw themselves into the production of material goods with that passion of which the human soul, destined for infinitude, is capable. Technics was merely the means by which this insatiable desire for material goods could be, or seemed to be, stilled, because technics is capable of unlimited development. Once brought into action, this process of unlimited increase and expansion could no longer be controlled. The machine invented by man began to control man's will; whether he liked it or not he had to obey the logic of technical development. It was exactly as in Goethe's symbolic ballad, *Der Zauberlehrling*, about the spying apprentice who had found out his wizard master's magic word which summoned obedient spirits to his service. For a while he revelled in the service of the water-carrying spirits; but before long he became afraid, because the spirits could no longer be controlled, so that by their very service the poor apprentice was in peril of being drowned—*Die ich rief, die Geister, werd ich nun nicht los*—a catastrophe from which the master's intervention saved him. This is very like our situation. Man has learned to control the immeasurable powers of nature. Modern man dominates nature to a degree unthinkable in previous ages. But whilst man controls nature by technics he no longer controls his own technics, but is more and more dominated by it and threatened with catastrophe.

Last century saw the climax of technical enthusiasm and of belief in progress by technics. It was then that people hoped technics would relieve man of all impediments and troubles connected with his body. "Our saviour is the machine", ran a sentence in a German newspaper. This enthusiasm for technics can still take hold of peoples whose technical development has lagged behind that of Western Europe. It can develop the more where the ground is prepared by secularist thinking which recognises only earthly and material goods. In Western Europe, however, this enthusiasm has been followed by disillusionment, deep despondency and fear. The first part of the story of the *Zauberlehrling* is finished. The second part is in full process and, since the invention of the atomic bomb, is approaching its climax.

Such disillusionment and despair might bring about a real turn of the pendulum in the right direction, but only if man is capable of understanding something of the deeper causes of this fatal, automatic development of technics, if he comes to see the false order of means and ends—that is, secularisation, loss of faith in God and in eternal values—as the root of the whole matter. All other proposals to make technics subservient again to human ends, and all attempts to heal the damage to social and personal life produced by the technical revolution, are mere palliatives. I do not mean that they are worthless, they may even be necessary, as the treatment of symptoms—such as fighting the fever—is often necessary until more radical therapy can begin. But unless there is a basic conversion, technics will develop as before, and the tempo of its development will not decrease but increase, because nowadays men not only make inventions but have found the technique of making inventions.

For this reason, all corrections coming from outside always come too late. The crazy tempo of technical revolution can only be reduced to a degree which is socially and personally supportable, if the whole scale of values of European nations can be changed. As long as material values indisputably take the first place, no change for the better is to be expected.

The perversion of the order of means and ends was caused by the decay of the consciousness of personality. And this in its turn was the consequence of the decay of Christian faith. In our time many have come to see, and are ready to admit, that moral values ought to be put in the first place. This insight is good, but not sufficient. Mere ethics has never displayed real dynamic. You cannot cure a demon-ridden technical world with moral postulates. In contrast to mere ethics and morality, Christian faith has the dynamic of passion, of surrender and sacrifice; it is capable of turning men to the eternal end, of unmasking demonic sin and thereby banning it, which no enlightened education is capable of doing.

Technics in itself is no problem for the Christian man. As long as technics is subordinate to human will, and human will is obedient to the divine will, technics is neutral, and as a means of goodwill is itself good. From the Christian point of view, there is no reason to condemn the machine and to return to the spinning-wheel. Even the use of atomic energy is not in itself harmful or bad. But we can hardly avoid the question whether technical evolution has not already passed the limits within which it is controllable by feeble, mortal men. This question cannot be theoretically decided. It is a question of the real dynamic. For us the only important question is whether mankind is ready, or may become ready, to perform that inward right-about-turn which alone will correct the fatal perversion of the order of means and ends.

II

SCIENCE

IF we are to ask what is the most characteristic feature of our epoch, we might wonder whether it is science or technics which gives the distinguishing mark to our time. Whilst to-day there is an obvious dependence between science and technics which makes the latter appear as applied science, it should be clear from the start that the unprecedented revolutionary development of technics in the middle of the 18th century had very little to do with science. Technics does not have its roots and origin in science, neither is it the scientific spirit which gave modern technics its incomparable dynamism. Technics springs from the will to dominate nature and to extend the power of man. If we are aware of this character of technics, it may become very doubtful whether it will be science or technics that will win the race that is taking place between the two in our time. It does not seem altogether impossible, or even improbable, that science may come more and more under the domination of technics, which is to say that the independent quest for truth may be transformed into a quest for the useful, as has already happened in countries where technocracy has become the state religion.

Whilst technics has been in existence in all times and in all countries—since man cannot but prove himself as *homo faber*—science is a late-comer in human history; and whilst all civilised nations of olden times reached a high standard of technics, there are only a few of them that have produced science. Technics originates from the necessities of life; it is, so to say, vitality in the realm of intellect. Science, however, in its essence is a decidedly non-pragmatic, " disinterested " activity, and for that reason much more spiritual than technics. It originates from the will to know the truth. A certain amount of suspicion is aroused when, in a particular epoch, natural science holds the field unchallenged by any competition; for this may be an index that the interest in truth is already displaced, or at least biassed, by the technical will to dominate nature. What legitimises Greek science so unequivocally, and proves its nature as a pure science, is, first, the almost complete absence of any attempt to apply scientific results technically; and in the second place, the astounding parallelism in the development of the *Geisteswissenschaften* alongside of natural science. In this sense, the Renaissance may be called a true rebirth of the classical scientific spirit. In spite of a simultaneous sudden growth of technical interest, the Renaissance scientists were moved by a pure will and a magnificent passion for knowledge of the truth; and some of this purely scientific impulse was preserved until quite recent times. Again, this is proved by that astonishing parallelism in the development of the *Geisteswissenschaften* alongside, and in competition with, natural science.

This may be the right moment to draw attention to a peculiar linguistic fact which is not without importance from the point of view of spiritual history. Neither the French nor the English have a common word including both natural science and *Geisteswissenschaften*. History, literature and linguistics do not come under the heading of sciences but under that of arts or letters. Psychology and sociology are classed with philosophy, and jurisprudence stands by itself. The German mind has had the courage to make the concept of science cover all these fields of investigation, evidently because that which is common to all of them—the quest for truth—has been felt to be more important than the differences. This synthetic or synoptic view includes both obligation and danger: obligation to scientific rigidity and objectivity, and the danger of a false application of the categories of natural science within the field of *Geisteswissenschaften*. In itself however, this synthetic concept of sciences is a precious heritage of the best Greek scientific spirit and an invaluable pointer in the direction of pure science, which does not " squint " after practical use—a heritage which in the epoch of technics (when science is in danger of being completely dominated by usefulness) cannot be preserved too jealously.

Science takes its orders from truth; that is its deep, you may even say, its religious pathos and ethos. It is not by mere chance that in the period of positivist philosophy an attempt has been made to divert science from this orientation to truth and to discredit the very concept of truth. Even in the sphere of pure science—physics and even mathematics—the idea of usefulness or expediency was substituted for that of truth. The laws found by physics were no longer " true " but merely " expedient " formulations. It is one of the most gratifying developments within this most revolutionary science of our days that this compromise with the pragmatic mind of the time has been shaken off, and so the temptation to betray the purity of the scientific mind has been overcome. Science has decided to remain in the service of truth and not to exchange truth for expediency. This decision must have the most far-reaching consequences.

Our era, however, has made us familiar with even more dangerous possibilities. The dynamic heir of positivist philosophy, the totalitarian state, has taken hold of science and succeeded in making it serviceable to its own purposes: science has to take its orders from political power. It has to start from its ideological presuppositions and has to prove that they are correct. Whether these are the racial philosophy of the *Herrenvolk*, or the Marxian doctrine, makes no difference. In both cases it means the prostitution of science, which in the long run would mean its end. For a science robbed of its freedom, a science to which certain methods, axioms and results are prescribed, has ceased to be science; it is a mere caricature of science. The versatility, however, which so many scientists showed in letting themselves be won over for this new course, shows more clearly than anything else that science has its ethical presuppositions without which it degenerates. It is dangerous to speak of science in the abstract. There is no science, there are only men who do scientific work. Science therefore is a part of human life. That is why science has its ethical presuppositions.

Truth is a severe and jealous mistress. She suffers no squinting to the left or to the right, she demands unconditional faithfulness. There is a scientific discipline which is much more a matter of character than of intelligence, there is a scientific conscientiousness for which the control of others is a poor substitute. Maybe a scoundrel of genius might achieve important scientific results, but he will do so only because he fits in with a structure of methods, standards, checks and tests which are produced and applied by a multitude of other scientists who are no scoundrels. It is true that personal ambition has played, again and again, an important rôle within the scientific process. But, where it is not controlled and checked by the capability and willingness to sacrifice personal prestige for the sake of truth, it has proved a severe hindrance to scientific progress. On the other hand, one of the most awe-inspiring traits of the true scientist is his willingness to acknowledge as erroneous what hitherto he has maintained as true, the willingness to subordinate personal fame to objectivity. Whilst it is true that ambition is a powerful stimulus of indefatigable research, the greatest achievements of science do not spring from ambition. They are the result of a genuine passion for truth. Again, the attempt has been made to substitute for this passion for truth mere curiosity. Certainly, curiosity is an important motive within the field of science. But taken by itself it is not sufficient to explain all the sacrifices, self-discipline and persistence which alone produce the great scientific achievements. Likewise it is impossible to explain in terms of egoistic motives the mutual trust between scientists which present-day scientific organisation makes necessary. Only the one who feels himself pledged to truth, is himself capable of trusting his fellow scientists, and he alone will prove capable of attaining the highest measure of scientific productivity. Without this practical idealism, without the genuine love and reverence of truth, science is doomed to sterility.

In our days this deepest spring of the scientific spirit is hidden by an immense scientific mass-organisation. Thousands of researchers are combined within a colossal plan of co-operation and division of labour, for the purpose of developing our knowledge of nuclear processes. It is obvious that only a minority within these thousands are inspired by a genuine scientific ethos. The whole thing looks like an enormous business which the individual worker might easily exchange for another one. What is true of this specific section of physics is true to a certain extent of other branches of science. Organisation seems to take the lead. But, if you look more closely, you can easily observe that even this enormous " big business " within science is unthinkable without scientific ethos. You simply have to imagine that the majority of those taking part in these organisations are motivated by mere egoism, and devoid of all truthfulness and conscientiousness, to see the complete impossibility, in such conditions, of fruitful co-operation towards one end. Furthermore, it remains true even now: *Wenn Könige bauen, haben die Kärrner zu tun*,[1] i.e. it is the great individual scientist and not the organisation which does the pioneer work. After all, science remains the domain of the great solitary truth-seekers who, like Kepler, Galileo and Newton, are moved and inspired by a sacred reverence for truth.

It was St. Augustine who made the first attempt to relate the idealism of truth to the Christian idea of God. From the point of view of a genuine Biblical theology, Augustine's system may not be altogether sound, being a synthesis of neoplatonic, pantheistic speculation with revealed God-knowledge. His basic idea, however, that the God of revelation is the origin of all truth had to be accepted even by Biblicists like Luther and Calvin. Whoever says " Truth ", says " God ". It is the common conviction and tenet of all Christian theology that there is no other truth—whatever its content—than truth in God. Why is this so?

The first affirmation of the Christian creed is: " I believe in God the Father Almighty, Maker of Heaven and Earth ". True, this first sentence, like the rest of the Christian creed, is spoken on the basis of God's revelation in history, in Jesus Christ. The

[1] When Kings build—carters must work.

source of this knowledge of the Creator is the same as the source of the knowledge of God the Saviour. The first part of the Christian creed is not a sentence of natural theology. The Christian knows the Creator primarily not from creation but from His Word. However, it is the specific character of this first part of the creed that its content includes objects of our natural knowledge—Heaven and Earth—which as such are also objects of scientific investigation. God has created that nature, the forms and laws of which Natural Science investigates. He has created that man, body and soul, who is the common object of Natural Science and *Geisteswissenschaften*. He has created men and world in such a way that man is able by his God-given reason to know the world—and it is his God-given destiny to know it. Moreover, God has created the world and is immanent and present in it in such a way that man, in knowing the world, cannot but know something of God's power and wisdom. Knowledge of whatever kind, if only it is true knowledge, is therefore never something *merely* natural and worldly; being the act in which something God made is grasped according to divine destiny, it is in itself something holy, sacred. In so far as true knowledge exists, it is always at the same time natural and supernatural.

That is, from the point of view of faith, the reason why knowledge of truth, even the search for truth, has in itself that deep "pathos and ethos" which we find present in all genuine scientific research, and which we find, before all, a dominant motive with the pioneers of science. Therefore all science could be, and ought to be, a divine service, a reverent following the traces—*lineamenta,* as Calvin says—of God's creation. Behind the postulate of scientific objectivity we find nothing less than awe in the face of God's order. What the scientist discovers are materialisations of God's thought and will. Man is not mistaken but supremely right if he feels science to be a high, divine vocation closely linked up with his human dignity, a sacred cause which requires surrender, loyalty and obedience, a duty which is laid upon him and which he cannot forsake arbitrarily.

If we understand science in this fashion there can be no

conflict with faith. It is the same God who has created this world which we penetrate by our scientific endeavours, and who reveals Himself in history. The revelation of God in His Word does not make scientific research unnecessary or unlawful. The Word of God in Scripture is no divine text-book of astronomy or anthropology. God's revelation in His Word is given to us by men who lived in the pre-scientific ideas of their time. On the other hand, no science can ever hope to give us what God reveals in His Word, because the world can never disclose the secret of God's gracious Will, forgiving man his sin and promising him eternal life. Science and faith are on different planes, perhaps we may say on planes standing vertically at right angles to one another, and having therefore merely a common intersecting line. The revelation in Christ takes place in that world which science investigates, but this revelation cannot become an object of science. Therefore it is equally stupid not to believe in God for scientific reasons and to oppose science for reasons of faith. The battle between Christian theology and science, which has aroused so much bad feeling between the two, has proved to be a mutual misunderstanding, caused by an overstepping of limits, partly from the side of faith, partly from that of science. In principle this problem does not exist any longer, though in practice it may never cease to bother us.

But the world in which we live and which we know is not simply God's creation, because we ourselves are not simply the men whom God created. Between God's creation and ourselves lies a gulf, a catastrophe which Christian faith calls the fall of man into sin. Even the scientist within his own sphere experiences the repercussions of this catastrophe. He does so in his ever-repeated experience that the scientific man accomplishes his service of truth less faithfully and reliably than he ought to, that he is often led by motives which are unfavourable to the knowledge of truth. Egoism, vanity, lust for power, partisanship of all kinds, are well known to have played an important rôle in scientific life. But the effects of sin within the scientific world are even deeper, so that they are hidden from moral commonsense. Man as a sinner is estranged from God, and so his sense of truth is poisoned at its very root. In the same place where St. Paul speaks of God's revelation in His created Work, he also lays his finger on this sore spot, that man in his sinful illusions confounds creation and Creator. He calls God what is not God. He absolutises what is not absolute. Again—and this is the aspect which is most important in the history of science— he simply forgets God and ignores the divine truth. All these possibilities, of which we have merely sketched an outline, have been realised in scientific progress and played fatal rôles: false absolutes—we might call them the pseudo-scientific myths —relativism, the illusion of positivism, that is, independence of all metaphysics. From the Christian point of view all these are equally manifestations of the one deep perversion of the mind which must pervert and deflect the course of science.

With the last remarks we touch upon the problem which the German calls scientific *Voraussetzungslosigkeit,* i.e. the postulate that the scientist must have no presuppositions. If by that we mean that scientific investigation must not be tied to any preconceived results but has to be completely open to the facts, whatever the facts may be, this postulate is identical with the idea of scientific inquiry as such. It is the postulate that science takes its orders from truth. But if by that postulate we mean to say that the scientist, in order to be a true scientist, must not have religious beliefs, such an axiom proves to be a mere prejudice which has nothing to do with science. This kind of *Voraussetzungslosigkeit,* just as the similar idea of indifference to value, is neither possible nor desirable.

For the scientist it is no gain but a loss if he does not believe in truth, the quest for which is a sacred service. That practical idealism which makes the scientist capable of sacrifice, that deep religious "pathos and ethos" which, as we have seen, is the characteristic of the greatest pioneers of science, is a potent motive and a directing force. It is the best, and perhaps the only sufficient, guarantee for an unconditional, genuine search for truth, and therefore for true scientific progress. Let us remember how, in the era of positivist philosophy, the substitution of utility for the idea of truth has endangered scientific activity. Much more do we see, in our era of technocracy and totalitarianism, how destructive the effect of utilitarianism and the loss of scientific ethos must be. There is, however, no truer, no purer " pathos and ethos " than the one which flows out of the Christian idea of God. Only those who cannot grasp the profound difference between faith-knowledge and scientific knowledge will believe that Christian faith anticipates replies to scientific questions and thereby destroys the necessary openness of the scientific mind.

But the positive contribution of faith to science is more than that. On closer inspection that metaphysical *Voraussetzungslosigkeit* or " neutrality " or " indifference ", which the positivist postulates, is no real possibility. He who does not believe as a Christian cannot help believing in something. That assumed neutrality proves to be a phantom, something which neither is nor can be. The metaphysical dimension of the mind never remains empty, but must always have a content. If it is not the Christian faith, then it is some kind of alternative metaphysics which is much more dangerous for science, being unconscious. Metaphysical neutrality simply does not exist, because neutrality in itself is a kind of sceptical metaphysics.

It is not surprising, then, that during the last centuries, when rationalistic philosophy and materialism took hold of the Western mind, we see within the field of science the appearance of certain axioms which seemed to be self-evident, but which were nothing but hidden, unconscious metaphysics: partly idealistic, partly materialistic. Such an axiom was the pan-causalism of the 18th century, the idea of Laplace, of a universal world-mechanics. A similar axiom took hold of the 19th century science: pan-evolutionism, i.e. the extension of the Darwinian principle of selection to the totality of phenomena, particularly to history. In general, we see a tendency to apply certain categories, which have proved helpful and even necessary in certain areas of science, to others by the sheer impetus of a monistic conception of Truth and Being. Wherever Christian faith was alive, these tendencies were powerfully resisted, but this was the exception, the movement of the time going in the opposite direction. At no time has this pseudo-scientific, monistic tendency dominated in a more dictatorial and uncritical way than in the era of positivist philosophy under the disguise of the slogan of metaphysical neutrality. What presented itself as metaphysical neutrality was, as a matter of fact, blunt naturalism, not to say stupid materialism: a preconceived axiom of the unity and uniformity of all phenomena. Of course this *is* metaphysics, metaphysics of the worst type. Instead of a true openness of mind not prejudicing the character of Being, we have here a metaphysical dogma of the uniformity of all Being, which proved to be genuinely harmful in the field of *Geisteswissenschaften* and contributed no little to the sad condition of the present world. I only mention a naturalistic sociology which abolished the notion of justice and introduced, instead, the principle of the survival of the fittest.

The postulate of the *Voraussetzungslosigkeit* proves to be misleading also from the point of view of epistemology. No science can work without *Voraussetzungen* (in Greek: hypothesis). Science gets answers only if it asks questions, and questions are alternative presuppositions. True scientific openness of mind does not consist in having no presuppositions but in having intuitively the right presuppositions in the form of questions or hypothetical answers. Only where the right questions are asked, that is, where the right hypotheses are intuitively introduced into the field of research, is new knowledge gained. Natural Science failed to progress as long as it was dominated by Aristotelian categories taken from the realm of man. On the other hand, where man and his history are subjected to the categories of Natural Science the results will be meagre, and in part pseudo-scientific. It so happens that man *is* different from his surrounding nature. Similarly, whoever were to use merely mechanical presuppositions in his study of organic life, would miss his object, because it so happens that the mechanical and the organic *are* different. Whoever works with a preconceived dogma of the uniformity of Being cannot but do wrong to some part of reality.

If once the false metaphysics, lying at the root of this monistic conception and the axiom of metaphysical neutrality, is seen as erroneous, the road is open for a further insight which throws a new light on the importance of Christian faith for true science. I am speaking of the knowledge of man, who is evidently a very specific, unique object of knowledge. He is unique for the reason that he is at the same time both the object and the subject of that knowledge, being the subject of all knowledge and science. Man is not merely one amongst the objects, because all knowledge, everything which we know of the world and nature, has its seat within man's mind. If I am not mistaken, it is exactly the most objective of all sciences—mathematical physics—which has reached a point where this indissoluble connection of subject and object has become evident in an overwhelming manner. Amongst all objects, man is the one who is always both object and subject at the same time. That is the deeper reason why the so-called *Geisteswissenschaften*, since they have to do with human history and the products of the human mind, have a structure so different from Natural Science that, as we have seen, Frenchmen and Englishmen prefer not to call them sciences.

The more deeply we penetrate into the being of man, the more clearly does it appear that the specifically human—that which is his alone—is the fact that he transcends himself. What we call culture is a product of man's self-transcendence. So is science. Man wants to know the truth; that truth reveals itself to him only in parts, in fragments, and therefore he must remain critical with regard to the results of his investigations; he must be ready to correct them. The mainspring of all this self-criticism is his passion for absolute truth; not a single fragment of knowledge is gained, as Planck has reminded us, if absolute truth is not aimed at. All science lives on this perspective of absolute truth. It is by this perspective that we can say: this is merely relatively true. Whoever says " relative ", must first have said " absolute ". This is the self-transcendence of man as it manifests itself in science.

Now, the most important manifestation of this self-transcendence is that act by which man transcends not only all he knows, but his very being, in subjecting *himself* to the judgment of ultimate truth. *That* he does this is one thing, *how* he does it is another. Which is that Truth to which he subjects himself in the totality of his being? This question, inevitable as it is, carries us beyond the range of mere knowledge into the sphere of faith. It cannot be answered without personal decision. The Christian believer does this in a manner different from the rest. The truth to which he subjects himself and by which he feels himself judged is unique in two features: in the radical nature of this judgment and in its thoroughly personal character. The believer knows that only by knowing God truly, does he know himself truly. That is why the Christian believer has a knowledge of himself different from all the others: he knows himself as a creature which is responsible to the Creator, and which at the same time lives in contradiction to his God-given destiny. Furthermore, he knows himself as a creature whose destiny it is to live in the Divine Love offered to him in the revelation of Divine Truth.

It is easily understood that the exploration of human history and of the specifically human manifestations, such as language, culture, state, law and so on, must lead to different results according as the explorer uses as his working hypothesis this Christian conception of man, or does not use it. Within the scientific process he uses this Christian view of man merely as a working hypothesis, ready to correct it, if his object makes it necessary. But the conflict between him as a believer and as a scientist never takes the form of an ultimate alternative, because it so happens that the Christian view of man proves itself to be the only realistic one, that is, the only one which stands the test of experience and does not falsify the picture of human reality. Whilst it is true that the Christian view of man gets its accurate form only in the process of critical scientific research, and many of the traditional formulations have to be sacrificed, it proves itself a key, opening doors which remain closed to any other.

The Christian conception of man produces also a certain view of the place of science within the totality of human existence, namely that science, however important, has no legitimate claim to the first place. Science knows what is, it does not know what ought to be. Science is a part of human destiny, but it is not this destiny itself, simply because it refers to what is and does not refer to what ought to be. Science is human, but it is not *the* human. Isolated from the totality of human destiny, or put into the first place dominating the rest, it kills the human centre, making men inhuman. It destroys personality, responsibility and love. Science is not bound to have this fatal result; it *does* have this result only if it usurps the first place, which does not belong to it.

Speaking in general, science in our day claims more room within the totality of human life than it is entitled to. Instead of serving, it dominates; instead of subordinating itself, it wants to subordinate the whole of life; that is why it has, in part, dehumanising effects. This is not the fault of science, but of man misunderstanding the function of science and giving it an importance which it should not have. It is not from science that we have to learn what is the task of man and what is the meaning of his existence. These are questions which lie outside the range of science, in the sphere of faith. Science is related to truth, but science is not the only way to truth. What science can know is a certain aspect of truth. The all-including Truth is God, and God is not an object of scientific knowledge. He is not an object at all, being the absolute subject, the one who has destined us, created relative subjects, for Himself and made us responsible to Him. Being the absolute subject, He never can be grasped by us. If we know Him, it is because He reveals Himself to us. When this happens—when the light of His truth enlightens and grasps us—then we begin to understand Him as the meaning of human existence and as the source of that deep "pathos and ethos" which is the life of genuine science.

III

TRADITION AND RENEWAL

CERTAINLY nobody would claim that our age is suffering from an overemphasis on tradition. Since the struggle against the *ancien régime*, particularly since the French Revolution, the western world has undergone a process of dissolution of tradition. The one example of England, however, proves that it is not merely the *inertia* of the forces then released which accounts for the continuation of this process. England, too, had its revolution, but after its successful accomplishment, the life of this island people re-established continuity with the previous tradition and never lost it in the following centuries. Within the rest of the western world there were always forces acting in an anti-traditional sense after the removal of the *ancien régime*.

The main force was rationalism. Continental Europe and the United States have experienced the effect of enlightenment much more deeply than Great Britain. Rationalism, the principle of enlightenment, is anti-traditional, for tradition does not belong to those "clear and perspicuous ideas" in which, since Descartes, the enlightened individual believes. The main argument of tradition—it was so, therefore it shall remain so—is offensive to modern man. What he cannot justify here and now in the light of reason does not put him under any obligation. The motive force of equality also works in the opposite sense from that of tradition. We people of to-day are equal to those who were before us. Therefore we have as much right to decide for ourselves what shall be and what shall not be, as they had in their time. By their reason men are essentially equal and alike. That which is unlike is unessential and should not be considered as essential. So tradition has no precedence over what seems to us better to-day. Tradition is essentially an aristocratic and not a democratic principle. In a world in which democracy, in the sense of equality, has become a kind of religion, tradition can neither be kept nor be formed. This is one of the main causes of the instability of western society during the last two centuries.

For tradition, rightly understood, plays the rôle of a firm scaffolding amongst the forces which create and carry the cultural life. Tradition means continuity, the element of duration and of persistence. The Latin word, *tradere*, means " to pass on "; those of the older generation pass on to the younger what they have received themselves. Tradition is inheritance, first in the very banal economic sense. Where there is no passing on of material values from father to son and grandson, there tradition in a spiritual sense will hardly persist. Culture presupposes continuity within its material foundation. Where the State by death duties and other taxation destroys this material continuity, it will also in the long run destroy the sense of spiritual tradition.

Tradition is, so to speak, cultural memory, the living preservation of the past in the present. Therefore tradition and the historical sense are closely connected. Where there is no love for the past, living tradition becomes impossible. The two merge imperceptibly: the passing on of historical memory and the passing on of values from the past generation to the coming generations. In order to pass on what has been, one must know it. Behind both, historical interest in the past and the passing on of values from the past, there is the same conception of the unity of the generations across the change of time, the solidarity between the present and the past. Only where the past is considered as ours—as something which belongs to us just as much as that which shall be to-morrow—can these two elements coexist: reverence for what past generations have done and the consciousness of guilt. To acknowledge guilt means to consider the past as a living presence. Where tradition and historical interest become weak, the consciousness of guilt also becomes weak.

With these reflections we have already touched the Christian view of tradition. The principle of tradition is deeply rooted in the Christian conception of life. The connection with those who were before us is guaranteed by the idea that all mankind is bound together with solidarity in creation and in sin. All of us are one in "Adam". We cannot forget that "Adam's" creation and destiny are ours. We cannot disconnect ourselves from "Adam's" guilt. All mankind has a common inheritance of creation and of sin. In the Christian message history is of capital importance. It is not surprising, then, that tradition is the very essence of the Christian Church. *Paradosis* is one of the key words of the Bible. To pass on what God has done and given to the previous generations is one of the most sacred duties of the Old Testament community. The Roman Catholic Church is right in affirming the capital importance of tradition. It is not on this point that the Reformation broke away from it; the break took place on the question whether or not the New Testament should be the norm of this tradition. But, in any case, the Christian Church lives by the passing on of historical revelation. The Church is a living continuity of past revelation, across the change of time.

Because the Church in her very essence is holy tradition, she also is the legitimate guardian of all natural and cultural tradition. This function she exerted, though imperfectly, in that epoch of tremendous break-down, when the Graeco-Roman cultural tradition was about to be lost. She performed the same function of guardianship throughout the Middle Ages, in the Greek Orthodox Churches and in the Churches of the Reformation, passing on the cultural inheritance at a time when respect for the past was already vanishing. Certainly Christianity shares the credit for this with the Renaissance Humanism, which in a more direct manner restored the continuity with antique culture. It is customary to attribute to Renaissance Humanism rather than to the Christian Church the chief merit of having given classical antiquity its legitimate share of modern European civilisation. Upon closer inspection, however, we shall see two things: first, that Renaissance Humanism showed its strength not outside but inside the Christian stream of life; second, that this Humanism fell a prey to rationalism and finally decayed in proportion to its alienation from the Christian tradition. Humanism kept its cultural vigour only where it remained in contact with Christianity, for the decisive element of tradition, i.e. loyalty to the heritage of the past, does not lie within the principle of Humanism as such, but in the Christian view of history.

This apparent paradox may be illustrated by a fact of language. During the whole of the Middle Ages until the end of the 17th century, the Latin language was the universal means of communication between European nations. Whoever had a claim to education spoke Latin. In our present era of Babel-like confusion of language we look back upon this time with envy. Why is it that this living connection with antiquity was broken? There may be many answers to this question, but there is one which seems to have more truth than others, namely that the Humanists with the Ciceronian Latin of the scholars killed the medieval Latin which the Church had made the universal means of communication. Had we kept it, we might be capable now of breaking the national linguistic barriers, as was the case when Englishmen, Frenchmen, Italians and Spaniards followed the Latin lectures of the German, Albertus Magnus, at the Sorbonne.

Tradition is not merely keeping alive the spiritual heritage of the past. Even more important, because more closely connected with the personal and social character of man, is the continuity of social values, such as custom, law, civil institutions, family tradition, public spirit and virtue. We understand best the tremendous importance of social rootedness and stability if we start from its opposite, as it is represented in a large modern industrial city. Already the outward picture of such a modern mushroom growth, compared with a city of old cultural tradition, is characteristic. One cannot refrain from expressing the contrast in terms of " mechanism " and " organism ". There is nothing more ugly, soulless and inhuman on the face of this earth than a gigantic mushroom-city built up by the accidental conflux of large masses at a place of industrial opportunity. It is like a giant city of brick barracks entirely dominated by the principle of bare utility, of mere " lodging ", without any form, the Magna Carta of all true tradition. This commandment, on the other hand, presupposes that the older generation takes the responsibility for the coming one. The chain holding together the generations and so forming tradition is woven of respectful gratitude and far-sighted responsibility. The fifth commandment is, however, only part of the divine law. This law, standing above the change of time, guarantees stability against change. The same law which has bound the old, binds the young. That is why it is written on stone tables. It is meant to last for ever. Where the sense of the divine law as the basic order of life is alive, you need not be concerned about the power of tradition. Even within those nations to whom the divine law and order of creation were only imperfectly known, but who were loyal to what they knew, the continuity of tradition was solid and the chain linking the generations proved to be unbreakable. The divine order of creation and the divine law formulating it are the basis of natural tradition.

But now tradition, fundamental as it is, is not solely a positive value in the life of mankind. *Es erben sich Gesetz und Rechte wie eine ew'ge Krankheit fort* (Goethe).[1] The stable element can dominate in such a way that it kills. Life is renewal and human life, in particular, is creation of the new. Man is distinguished from animals just by the fact that he creates new things; that he does not repeat the same melody throughout the centuries, but invents new songs; that he does not reproduce the same pattern like the bee and the beaver. The element of creativity is inseparable from spirit and culture; it is new knowledge, new invention, the creation of something which has never been before. In order to create the new, one has to be independent of the old. One needs courage, love of adventure, to sail into the unknown dangers of the open sea. Here is the field for the pioneer who is not afraid to stand alone, to swim against the stream and to take a course hateful to the mass of those who are bound by tradition.

Nay, is not living tradition in itself renewal? *Was Du ererbt*

---

[1] Law and rights are handed down from generation to generation like a never-ending disease.

von deinen Vätern hast, erwirb es, um es zu besitzen (Goethe).[1] Living tradition is not merely transmission but a receiving and giving which on both sides is creative. Every live teacher is somehow an artist who, by teaching, releases the sleeping powers of the pupil, while a live pupil does not merely receive, but by appropriating forms something new. When tradition becomes mechanical reproduction, it is neither alive nor human. Genuine tradition is creative appropriation which in itself is progressive transformation. Live individuality cannot appropriate without giving, stamping with its own stamp. Appropriation means reception into the organic whole, which in itself is unique.

The creation of new things is necessary because what has been reached up to now is only a step on the long road to a distant end. The capacity to transcend himself, which is the very essence of man, is founded in the idea of perfection and absoluteness, with regard to which every achievement appears as a mere approximation which cannot ultimately satisfy. The restless reaching out after the new is not grounded merely in a desire for change but in this striving for the perfect and absolute which dwells in the human mind. The more inexorably each achievement is measured by the norm of perfection and absoluteness, the more alive is the spirit. The spirit is thus living in the unrest of a "not yet". This is the dynamic of the idea of progress. It might appear, then, that the intensity with which the idea of progress has moved the modern mind is a sign of the spiritual vitality of our age.

This would really be so if that "not yet" were the true expression of our relation to the perfect and absolute. This superficial evaluation of our human situation is, however, exactly that false optimism which was the reproach of the past century. To see our reality from the view-point of "not yet" is an optical illusion. Not only is our life not yet good, not yet human, but rather no more good and no more human. It is not merely incomplete with regard to the perfect, but it contradicts it.

This statement does not apply to all spheres in the same

[1] What thou hast inherited from thy fathers acquire it so as to possess it.

way. There are things which are imperfect or incomplete. The category of contradiction—or opposition—is meaningless, say, in the sphere of technical problems. The first locomotives were really imperfect compared with the present ones. In this sphere there is unambiguous progress. The same is true, although not in the same measure, of scientific knowledge. Science proceeds from the imperfect to a more and more perfect condition of knowledge. However, the category of "not yet" becomes most problematic in the moral sphere, and it becomes entirely wrong where the moral condition is viewed in connection with our God-relation. Our relation to God cannot be said to be "not yet" good. From the point of view of faith it is clearly "no more" good, that is, it is placed in the category of opposition or contradiction. Sin is not mere imperfection but deviation, opposition to the will of God, even destruction of the God-given status. The more man's understanding of himself becomes personal, the more the category of "not yet" becomes irrelevant. The fact of "opposition" is central, and progress is an unsuitable category in the Christian understanding of man's relation to God. Where man's true being is understood as communion with God, the judgment on our actual being is this: loss of communion, separation from God by sin and guilt. The only possible solution of the human problem is the restoration of the destroyed communion by forgiveness and salvation.

With the message of redemption in Christ and of ultimate salvation, a completely new element enters human life which also entirely reshapes the relation of tradition and renewal. The restoration of God-communion is perfected in Christ. We look back upon it as something past. "It is finished", once and for all. The knowledge of this divine achievement is entrusted to the Church, that she may pass it on from generation to generation. This passing on—this *traditio*—is her very essence and life. Church is tradition. On the other hand, what the Church passes on is something perfectly new, the unheard of novelty of divine forgiveness, gratuitous love and the promise of final salvation and perfection. The content of the Christian message and tradition are those things which "eye saw not, and ear heard not—prepared for them that love Him ". Jesus Christ is the " novissimum " of all history which cannot be derived from anything preceding, but which also remains the "novissimum" throughout all history. He is the end of all history, its transcendent goal; to believe in Him means also to believe in a new heaven and a new earth. "Behold, I make all things new", says He, who is the alpha and the omega, the beginning and the end.

That is why Christian faith, wherever it is genuine, is not merely a power for progress but a revolutionary force in history. Faith in Christ, in the One who started a new history, is at the same time renewal of human existence here and now. Christian faith is inseparable from new birth, from being a new creature. " Wherefore, if any man is in Christ, he is a new creature: the old things are passed away; behold, they are become new." This newness bursts asunder all continuity of tradition. Such novelty is not merely an improvement but a perfect revolution, a revolution of thought and will. In the New Testament the patterns of continuity are rejected in sharpest antithesis. The new man is opposed to the old man in blunt contradiction. In a radical right-about-turn man must break with the old and turn completely towards the new. Christian existence is radically revolutionary, being the expectation of the perfectly new world.

But what, then, of the necessity for tradition and conservation? We have to distinguish between centre and periphery. The New Testament faith is radically revolutionary in the centre, that is, in its relation to God and to men, but it is not at all revolutionary in the periphery. Neither Jesus nor the Apostles attack the state or the social order with the intention of replacing them by another order. Not even such an immoral institution as slavery is directly questioned. The revolution takes place at first in the personal centre only. This emphatic distinction between centre and periphery is such a marked feature of the new life in Christ that at first sight the community of early Christians might appear to be utterly conservative in the political, social and cultural spheres. If we recall, however, that little jewel of the New Testament, St. Paul's letter to Philemon, we see that this conservatism is merely apparent. This letter was addressed to a member of the Christian Church in Colossæ, recommending its bearer, a fugitive slave, to his master. Whilst St. Paul takes the institution of slavery for granted, he transforms it from within into a relation of brotherhood. A silent revolution takes place in the personal centre and from there transforms the social relationship.

We cannot understand such a relation between centre and periphery unless we bear in mind that the renewal through Christ is at the same time the restoration of the primeval good creation of God. Through Jesus Christ the image of God in man, which has been destroyed by sin, is restored. By the silent revolution the creatureliness of man is not ascetically negated, but completed or fulfilled. Nowhere is this more clearly to be seen than in the element which is so decisive for tradition: marriage and the family. Marriage is not denied but fulfilled through Christ by being made a symbol of the unity between Christ and His body. In a similar way the institution of the family is not dissolved but transformed from within by being made a symbol of the paternal filial relation between God and man.

This is to say that the radical revolution within the invisible centre creates a silent revolution in the visible periphery, not by changing laws, institutions and orders as such, but by inwardly transforming them and giving them a new meaning. That is why the most revolutionary force of world history manifests itself under the disguise of a conservative attitude. It is exactly by being so radically revolutionary, that it takes a conservative appearance. The Christian knows that all changes which begin from without are no real changes. For, after all, it is always man who makes the conditions and not the conditions that make men. Outward revolutions are therefore at bottom fictitious, much ado about nothing. Of course the world does not believe this. For the superficial mind, which fails to understand the real relation between centre and periphery, the silent revolutions always are too slow and not radical enough. It is only by becoming a Christian that a true valuation of the really revolutionary forces is gained; the secularised mind will always overestimate outward appearance and underestimate radical, inward change.

The true revolution, even within the social, political and cultural spheres, is always that which takes place within and seems to be conservative without. Certainly, there is a danger, lest the principle of inwardness become a mere disguise of unreality. This danger is, however, inseparable from the life of faith. Faith in the grace of God is always liable to be taken as a pretext for moral sloth and inertia. This, however, is not the fault of faith, but of its being misunderstood. Misunderstood faith can use the principle of inwardness as a disguise for a false conservatism, which preserves the present order not because of its element of divine creation but merely for reasons of personal privilege. All these misunderstandings cannot undo the truth that genuine faith, with its silent revolution, is an incomparably more radical transforming power than outward reformation and revolution.

This primacy of the "silent revolution" which is implied in the genuinely Christian distinction of centre and periphery does not, of course, exclude drastic action with a view to changing outward conditions and social structure. But two things will always distinguish the Christian from a secular revolutionary. First, structural changes will never be given first place because of their ambiguity and ambivalence. Though the motive behind them may be truly Christian, they may work out in a very different direction. The best of laws may create the worst of results if handled by men of evil spirit. Second, the Christian will not be in favour of outward changes before the situation is "ripe" for them. Otherwise such changes may produce more confusion than good, and, if they are not prepared from within, they will not last or will last only by tyrannical enforcement. That is why those social changes, which are the result of Christian motives, are more of an organic than of a violent nature. Radical as is the break between the old and the new in the centre, the change in the periphery—in outward conditions and structure—takes on rather the character of slow growth. Great Christians were never "revolutionary" in the ordinary sense of the word. The "revolutionary principle" in this sense is much more the product of equalitarian rationalism than of Christian faith. It is radically opposed to tradition whilst, in the Christian view of things, a high valuation of tradition is paradoxically united with an incessant push to renewal.

Modern man, who has emancipated himself from God's order and usurped the rights of God, has also made for himself the claim: "Behold, I make all things new". Having somehow become omnipotent in his dominion over nature, he thinks himself able to throw overboard all tradition and to create a perfectly new order according to his own design. This new order, however, always carries the stamp of technical rationality. As he overlays nature with his man-made, artificial second nature, by technical civilisation, so he also substitutes for already slowly developed culture an artificial, planned civilisation, which is as ugly and inhuman and destructive of real creativity as those mushroom cities of the late 19th century.

Christian faith alone is capable of combining tradition and renewal, because it is based upon the unity of God the Creator and God the Redeemer. Tradition alone leads to petrifaction; renewal alone leads to dissolution, artificial planning and tyrannical centralisation. The Christian faith affords the possibility and necessity of both: of reverent preservation and continuity and of radical change and indefinite growth. Both are equally necessary for a truly human civilisation.

One last thing must be said. Whilst it is true that the Christian faith lives by *paradosis*, by handing over the Gospel truth to every new generation, it is equally true that this handing over creates real living faith only where this tradition is capable of renewal itself. The Gospel truth is the same throughout all centuries. But the human interpretation of this truth must be new in every new epoch, and the forms in which this tradition takes place must be different, according to the times and circumstances. Mere traditionalism is the death of the Church, just as mere revivalism is its dissolution. So it is in the Church itself—in its functioning as the means of veritable tradition and renewal—that this duality of conservation and reformation has to take place. As a matter of fact, it is not two things but one thing. The Church has to give the world the living Word of the living God. It is by His living Word that God preserves the world, and it is by His living Word that He renews the world. Where this Word is alive and preached as a living Word, and where it is received in real faith, it cannot but do both: preserve what God wants to have preserved and renew what God wants to have renewed.

It is this mysterious unity of tradition and renewal which is the only hope in a world in which false conservatism and false revolutionism have brought about a tension which spells disaster. To enter into that mysterious unity of tradition and renewal is the meaning of the old and much abused word, conversion. And it is there where the mere exposition of thought has to stop and the decision of the individual has to come in.

IV

EDUCATION

THE cultural level of a country is often judged by the measure of education of its population. What is education? There is an aspect of education which is not specifically human. We know the adequate and at the same time touching exertions of animals in training their young ones in the arts of their life. Human education is a continuation of these exertions, by which the older generation introduces the younger generation into the habits and arts of their own life. Human education, then, is a form of tradition; its purpose is to pass on the experiences of the earlier generation, their convictions of what is necessary to life, their conception of values and standards, their habits and practices, and to train those who come after in all these. The subject of education is primarily the community: in the first place the family, but also the clan, and finally the political community. Education, like all tradition, is in its essence an activity of the community. In primitive societies education ends with a rite of reception into the community of the adult, by which act he now becomes responsible.

It was an event of revolutionary importance when Socrates for the first time proclaimed as the true purpose of education individual independence, spiritual self-reliance. His *maieutic* method aimed, as the name indicates, at simply drawing out, or bringing to the light of the day, what is hidden in every man. He therefore questions the principle of education that had been dominant hitherto, namely, its character of tradition. The Socratic teacher does not pass on; he does not give, but wants to make the pupil independent of anything given and of any giver.

The idea of education as evolution, development, was thus discovered. But this new individualistic idea was never accepted —either in the time of its first prophet, or later on—to such a degree as to displace the older idea, with its basis in social tradition. On the contrary, the Socratic method of education always remained an exception. The material weight of the things to be passed on and the necessity of social tradition was so great that the Socratic element of education was always confined within narrow limits.

All the same, there was even in the traditional idea an element somehow akin to the Socratic method, namely, the element of training, the development of those capacities and skills which seemed useful to the community. Training is different from passing on. Its aim is individual mastery. After all, even the act of passing on, of tradition, contains at bottom an element which we might call Socratic; appropriation of what is to be received. Wherever tradition is alive and not mechanical, this element of individual, active appropriation must be present. On the other hand, the Socratic idea has its limits. The mind or spirit cannot be educated or formed without offering it certain materials for self-active appropriation. The Socratic ideal was based on the *a priori* elements of that which dwells in the mind, and is therefore independent of history. Socratic education evidently has a rationalistic, anti-historical leaning.

It is obvious that Christianity introduced into the world an idea of education which—at first sight—is completely opposed to that of Socrates. In the Christian conception the historical is everything, the *a priori* nothing. Christianity is in itself *paradosis, traditio*, of historical revelation. Something divinely given has to be passed on. Furthermore, Christianity is essentially social. The individual has to be fitted into the Christian community and finally—and this seems to be the sharpest opposite to Socrates—the aim is not the self-active spirit or reason, but the acceptance of something given which is beyond reason. The victory of Christianity, then, seemed to carry with it—in its idea of education—the complete denial of the Socratic idea.

This was so much the case that even in the moment where western education began to emancipate itself from Christian leadership—i.e. in the Renaissance—this fundamental opposition was not yet felt. The return to antiquity did not take place at first in the direction of individual independence or autonomy, but as an appropriation of the antique cultural values as distinct from the Christian ones. Education was, in fact, so entirely conceived as passing on, that at this time the question was merely: what is to be passed on? It seemed to be possible to take over the cultural heritage of antiquity without thinking independently for oneself. But the masters of antiquity could not but create a spirit of independence and the courage of thinking for oneself. It could not be long before the specific character of Socratic education was rediscovered, and the idea of education as the development of the indwelling germs of the individual mind was given first place. Descartes' *Discours de la méthode*, with its regress upon the *a priori* certainties, and Leibnitz's *Monadology*, with its principle of the monad without window, gave the Socratic idea a new philosophical and metaphysical weight. Lessing's treaty, *Die Erziehung des Menschengeschlechts*, is important in two respects. First, Lessing is the first modern thinker who understood the whole history of humanity from the point of view of education, divine education, thus showing the way to Herder and German idealistic humanism. Second, Lessing tried to combine Christian revelation with the Socratic idea of education. He interpreted divine revelation as being a means of accelerating the development of the *a priori* possibilities lying in man's spirit. It was, however, Rousseau who, for the first time and in the most comprehensive manner, applied the Socratic ideal to the education of children and youth, and thus even surpassed Socrates. With Herder the idea of education as *Bildung*, i.e. organic development of all inward possibilities lying within man's nature, is magnificently based upon a universal conception of history. All human history is but one great process of spiritual development.

What German humanism since Herder understands by *Bildung* has no parallel in any other country or language. That is why the word cannot be translated. By a grandiose synthesis, Christianity was combined with the Socratic idea of education. What Goethe, Schiller, Humboldt, Fichte, Schleiermacher and Hegel understood by *Bildung* is a synthesis of historical tradition or communication and Socratic self-development. The product of this synthesis is the truly *gebildete Persönlichkeit*. This *gebildete Persönlichkeit*, the highest point man can reach, is an individual in whom all latent possibilities are fully developed by the appropriation of that which is given to him from outside, from nature and history. The whole wealth of historical heritage, of antiquity and Christianity, is here conceived of as a means of education. Education itself, however, is understood Socratically as self-development. History plays the rôle of the Socratic teacher. It is the stimulus that brings forth the development of inner wealth. Contrary to the rather polemic attitude of some of these thinkers with regard to Christianity, the decisive influence of Christian personalism appears in the fact that the idea of personality dominates within this system of education. Goethe's confession *höchstes Glück der Erdenkinder ist doch die Persönlichkeit* is not only his, but that of the whole classical epoch of German idealistic humanism.

Within this conception of *Bildung*, the idea of education has outgrown the limitations within which it was confined up to Lessing. Education understood as *Bildung* is not a process which is completed by reaching the age of maturity but one which only then comes to its own. *Bildung* is the real life of the man who is spiritually awake. It is the very essence of humanity to become a truly *gebildete Persönlichkeit;* it is the highest aim towards which man can strive, according to the Orphic word: "Become what Thou art". Education gains here a new meaning of immeasurable width and depth. Man is a microcosm containing and reflecting the macrocosm. He can and shall appropriate to himself the totality of nature and history. At the same time nature and history are meant to become united in his personality.

The idea of *Bildung* in German idealistic humanism is certainly one of the grandest and most beautiful achievements of the human mind. Although it was the life programme of a small *élite*, and although it was so ambitious that it could be shared only by men of high culture, it has exerted a great influence. From this ideal, the renewal of the German university (for which the newly created University of Berlin was the model) took its start. The schools of secondary education followed its example. The enthusiasm and the deep sense of responsibility, with which in this epoch the reform and extension of popular education were tackled, have their origin in the impulses which came from the spiritual heroes of Weimar, Jena and Berlin. The rôle which this spirit of education played in the national awakening of the German nation, leading to the War of Liberation against Napoleon, cannot be ignored. The influence which this powerful and high-minded philosophy exerted, far beyond the German frontiers, is well known. It had even a political effect in the democratic movement of 1848, which was unfortunately crushed by Bismarck.

All the same it was not by chance that in the political, as well as later in the social competition of forces, this movement came to an early end. The ideal of *Bildung* was, as we have already mentioned, too exclusively fitted to a spiritual *élite* and could not be adapted to the requirements of the common man. This is the decisive limitation of idealistic humanism. It was an educational ideal for spiritual heroes; it could never become popular. The adaptation of this conception of education to primary schools and family education proved to be impossible. It is true that the school programmes, with a few phrases originating from this realm, proclaimed beautiful things about the development of the total personality. As a matter of fact, in the real school education these phrases remain on paper, whilst actual education and training follow quite different, more practical, lines.

Fortunately, there existed and still exists another much older idea of education, which is capable of being the basis of all, even the most popular, education: the Christian idea. This Christian idea of education, however, was never clearly conceived and worked out. In the Church of the first centuries, Christian education was limited to baptismal instruction, containing the elements of Christian doctrine and ethics, combined with family tradition. How this Christian family tradition and ethics grew up we do not know. We do know, however, that it must have been very efficient in the first centuries, because otherwise the continuous growth of the Christian Church could not be understood. Christian personalities were trained who stood the test of life. The Christian idea of education was not worked out, because obviously this was not necessary. The passing on of Christian doctrine and morality, and the training for Church and family life, were sufficient. The first part,, doctrinal instruction, was performed according to the didactic rules prevalent in the synagogue and in existing schools. The second part was performed, so to say, instinctively.

The same is true, more or less, of the Middle Ages. For the simple Christians the catechism and Church custom seemed sufficient. For the more ambitious, there were the higher and highest schools of learning with their combination of Christian theology, philosophy and liberal arts. But for both, the simple people and the spiritual *élite*, a large part in education was played by the Sacraments, which accompany the whole life from birth to death, and which at that time were observed daily. No doubt, the Church of the Middle Ages did a tremendous work of education by its religious apparatus and by its effective endeavour to permeate the whole of life by its sacramental practices. No wonder, then, that in this epoch the conflict between Christian theology and the Socratic idea of education did not become acute. The lack of a formulated Christian idea of education was covered by the actual educational work of the Church.

This lack, however, became much more dangerous in the Churches of the Reformation. Here the sacramental training and Church habits were reduced to a minimum. On the other hand, preaching and teaching the doctrine of the Bible was pressed almost exclusively. These two facts together created an enormous educational vacuum. Whilst in theological knowledge the New Testament origins of Christianity were rediscovered, it was almost completely forgotten that the original Christian Church was before all a living community, that the Holy Spirit worked primarily by means of communal life, and that at that time the younger generation received their Christian influence and instruction not merely through preaching and teaching but through training in Church life. The educational vacuum, which became more and more obvious, is primarily due to the lack of capacity and even of endeavour on the part of the Reformation Churches to develop a Christian community life. Certainly, there exists a considerable difference between Lutheran and Calvinistic Churches. Calvinism, and even more the sects deriving from Calvinism, have paid much more attention to the formation of living communities than the Lutheran and even the Zwinglian Churches, where the identification of Church and civic community worked in the opposite direction. But the tendency towards orthodox intellectualism developed the same vacuum even within the Calvinistic Churches. The orthodox intellectuals' emphasis on doctrine is the main cause of the educational vacuum of Protestantism.

It is true that the intellectualist misunderstanding of faith—identifying faith with belief in doctrines—was a tragedy in the Christian Church, that had already begun in the second century. But up to the time of Protestant orthodoxy this fatal onesidedness was compensated to a certain extent by intensive ecclesiastical training and habit. Whilst the Reformation in its centre was the rediscovery of the non-intellectualist conception of faith, this new discovery was lost all too soon in the fight against the Roman heresy. The Reformation Churches became orthodox. The old intellectualist misconception of faith became dominant again, but was now much more dangerous than in the Catholicism of the Middle Ages, because all those compensatory elements, by which the Church of the Middle Ages had covered its bareness, were now lacking. Once Church doctrine, theology and catechism had acquired their almost monopolistic position, education was reduced to theological teaching. No doubt, even within Protestantism, Christian custom played its rôle and Christian training was an element of family life. But these elements were secondary and not sufficiently connected with a truly evangelical community life. The resentment against Roman Catholic training resulted in discrediting training as such.

We have to mention another factor of great importance—the fight of Reformation theology against the opinion that man could co-operate with God in things of faith led to a conception of revelation which stood in opposition to the Socratic idea. Orthodox theological doctrine, as expressed for instance in some Lutheran Confessions, interpreted in mechanical terms the exclusive divine activity in the conversion of men. The active element of appropriation was eliminated. If you study the classical catechisms of the 16th and 17th centuries, which in many respects are masterpieces, you will see that the activity of the pupil is reduced to a minimum. The doctrine that the human mind to which faith is imparted is a *truncus et lapis*, has devastating effects upon teaching. The ordinary catechism instruction is an educational monstrosity.

From this point of view, the Socratic revolution, beginning with Descartes and leading on to German idealism, was an historical necessity and an indubitable gain. Here the pupil is at last taken seriously as an active factor in learning. Against the background of orthodox passivism, one can understand the tremendous impression made by the educational ideas of the 18th century, and also the energy and passion with which the orthodox system was attacked. Protestantism, in spite of its priceless Biblical insight, has led to an educational debâcle which would have become much more apparent had not the revival of teaching in the 18th century and 19th century been carried on in the name of Protestantism.

Up to the present day, the Christian idea of education has not been fully worked out. In that respect, Reformation theology, even in its best forms, has proved unsatisfactory, because it was never capable of combining the necessary Socratic element of active appropriation with the Christian conception of divine revelation. There are, however, two great exceptions to this negative general statement, two thinkers at least who have made most valuable contributions toward a Christian idea of education: the great Swiss educator, Pestalozzi, and the great Danish Christian thinker, Kierkegaard.

In general, Pestalozzi has been misunderstood as being a follower of Rousseau and of German idealism, though, as a matter of fact, the basis of his pedagogical system is emphatically Christian. It is true that Pestalozzi took over from Rousseau the idea of self-development, and worked out his pedagogical message according to the Socratic principle of development of the germs lying in man. In that respect he is at one with the main trend of the time. On closer inspection, however, we see an unbridgeable gulf between Pestalozzi's guiding principles and those of Rousseau and the German humanists. This appears already from the basic fact that the central idea in Pestalozzi's system is the Christian idea of love. Education for him is education in love and for love. He is in complete disagreement with his contemporaries, and in complete agreement with the Christian tradition, in putting the main emphasis on the education by the family, particularly by the mother, and in subordinating all education to the one belief that men become human by living in the love of God and in loving communion with their fellow men. Again he is thoroughly Christian in emphasising the dignity of manual work and the unity of man's body and spirit. Pestalozzi, in spite of his idealistic terminology, is a Christian prophet of humility, social responsibility, and life in prayer, deeply rooted in Biblical revelation and tradition. He has learned whatever was to be learned from his idealistic contemporaries and their idea of *Bildung*, but the basis of his instruction is neither Rousseau nor German idealism but Biblical faith.

It is greatly to be regretted that the Christian Church and theology were prevented by intellectualism from understanding the unique importance of this first great Christian philosopher of education, and that they left it to the epigoni of German humanism to develop and to propagate Pestalozzi's ideas in a direction foreign to the intentions of the master. A genuine Christian conception of education could have been gained from Pestalozzi, or at least developed, for he was the first thinker who had tried to combine the Socratic idea of self-development and spontaneous appropriation with the Christian faith in divine revelation. After what we have seen about the fatal misunderstanding of orthodoxy in the matter of appropriation of divine truth, we certainly cannot seriously blame Pestalozzi for lacking in orthodoxy.

It may seem rather astonishing that we should speak of Sören Kierkegaard in this connection, because this great thinker does not seem to have been very much interested in the problem of education. We are justified, however, in mentioning him here, because the dominant problem of his philosophy is the relation between the Socratic conception of learning and Christian faith and because his main interest was the truly active *appropriation* of the Christian message. Hence, we can understand his sentence: " The subject is the Truth ". This sentence, expressing better than anything else what he was after, is not an expression of romantic subjectivism, of Fichte's philosophy of the " Ego ", nor of Cartesian rationalism; it is spoken simply out of his concern for genuine " existential " faith as distinguished from orthodox belief in a creed. Kierkegaard, however, has met with the same fate as Pestalozzi: the Church and the theologians failed to understand him.

Kierkegaard's doctrine of the paradox, of the scandal, of the existential character of faith, has certainly exerted considerable influence on recent theology. But his doctrine of appropriation, which is at the root of all his dialectic, has not been understood, has not even been noticed. So far as Protestant theology is concerned, it did not fit in with the conceptions of sin and grace, as they were formulated by Reformation theology. The doctrine of *sola gratia* did not seem to leave room for Kierkegaard's concern for active appropriation. Protestant theology is still dominated by a mechanistic conception of God's activity in conversion. And this is precisely why Protestantism up to this hour has not been able to develop a Christian idea of education, and to relate Christian faith to the different spheres of autonomous cultural life.

In their time, the Reformers had tried to solve this problem by making a distinction between Christian revelation on the one hand and secular science and arts on the other. By this simple distinction they were capable of combining with their theology a rather generous estimate and use of cultural values of the Graeco-Roman civilisation. In spite of Luther's fight with Erasmus and of Castellio's expulsion by Calvin, all the great

Reformers were also humanistic admirers of classical antiquity. This is particularly true of Zwingli and Calvin. Whilst their theology differed greatly from that of the humanists, they shared with them not merely their love of Greek and Latin, but also their high estimate of classical literature, poetry, philosophy, political science and science in general, so long as the question of free will did not interfere. But they left unsolved or even untouched the problem, to what extent Christians could and should learn from the pre-Christian pagan masters and left undefined the limit of what was or was not admissible. We certainly cannot blame them for not being capable at the same time of reforming Church and theology and of solving the problem of the relation between Christianity and secular culture. They had undoubtedly done enough; their followers, however, did not have the necessary calibre to tackle the task which the great masters had left behind. On the one hand, they turned back to the medieval synthesis; on the other hand, they developed a narrow-minded Biblicism on the basis of verbal inspiration, which could not but lead to a severe conflict with science and to the cultural impoverishment of the Protestant world. The lack of a Christian conception of education was a serious handicap.

This vacuum, however, became fatal directly Cartesian rationalism and German idealism produced the new and inspiring idea of *Bildung* [1] and when the 19th century, compelled by the development of natural science and modern industry, forced modern mankind to face entirely new problems. Whilst in the time of the great German idealists, history and classical antiquity were the primary material from which the education of the *gebildete Persönlichkeit* was expected, the demands now became much more realistic and practical. Nature took the place of history; the social and political problems and struggles of the present displaced the interest in antiquity. National consciousness superseded idealistic cosmopolitanism; the claims of state and society left little room for the development of personality. A new idea of education, originating from a

[1] Culture.

naturalistic theory of evolution and from pragmatism, took the place of the two older traditions—the Christian and the idealistic. Education was now conceived as an adaptation to the social environment.

The American philosopher, Dewey, was the first to formulate this new realistic idea of education on the basis of a naturalistic evolutionism. The extraordinary success which Dewey's educational programme had, even amongst those who did not agree with his naturalistic philosophy, is due in no small measure to the fact that he drew, more or less unconsciously, from humanistic and even Christian reserves. It is probable that even the great example of Pestalozzi had its share in his educational conceptions.

This is now our educational situation: a chaotic mixture of the most varied traditions and ideas: medieval and Protestant Christianity, Rousseau, German idealism, pragmatic naturalism, Marxist economic materialism, nationalism and political totalitarianism. The question is whether Christianity is capable of producing a conception of education which can combine with the highest claims of Christian personalism the Socratic element of self-development on the one hand, the new insights of natural science and the practical requirements of economic and political life on the other.

If we answer this question with a confident " yes ", we do not mean by this that this idea has already taken shape in our mind, but only that our understanding of the Christian faith makes it possible. We agree with the 18th century humanists that the idea of personality must be in the centre of education. But it is just in the understanding of personality that the roads part. From the point of view of Christian faith, personality is not something given, which only needs development, but it is a relation. Personality is rooted in the relation to God. It is that " self " of man which is called into existence by the divine " Thou ". Its centre is responsibility, understood as the response of man to God's call. Its true realisation, and therefore true humanity, is existence in divine love becoming concrete in love towards our neighbour. This is Pestalozzi's idea of education.

We must, however, distinguish more clearly than he did between the divine calling to this existence and an innate possibility. This possibility does not lie in man. It cannot be developed; it must be given. But Pestalozzi is right, against his orthodox critics, in maintaining that this personality does not come to existence without man's highest activity; it is not thrown into man, but man is called to it, so that nobody can take away his own responsibility. Out of this conception of personality a new educational programme can and must be developed, combining the Socratic element of self-development with the Christian concept of divine grace.

All the powers and possibilities of mind and body, which are in man and which can and must be developed, are placed in a new relationship and unity by this central act, by which true personality is created. They are not denied but transformed. Nobody becomes a genius by faith. Mathematical or physical knowledge is not upset by the fact of conversion. There exists a certain autonomy of the powers of reason, imagination and feeling, given by the Creator, which have to be respected so long as they are not absolutised. These powers then have to be developed according to their own law, and this is the place of the Socratic element. But it is no more than an acknowledgment that all these powers are gifts of the Creator and subordinate to the highest personal and communal destiny of man, as it is given by the Christian faith, which can prevent them from anarchic competition with each other and unify them harmoniously. Furthermore, the development of innate powers has to take account of the fact that man is a sinner and that nothing in him is exempt from the destructive effects of sin. In this respect, however, a fundamental law has to be considered. The more peripheral or extraneous a sphere of life, i.e. the further it is removed from the personal centre, the less does the question of sin come in. It would be hard—though not impossible—to discover the difference between a pagan or atheist and a Christian mathematics, but we can certainly distinguish most clearly between a Christian and a non-Christian conception of freedom, of moral obligation, of marriage and family, because in all these questions the sinful " Ego " of man plays its rôle. The reformers were undoubtedly right when they were inclined to learn from Aristotle's logic but were rather sceptical concerning his ethics; they were right in enjoying classical poetry and at the same time criticising its pagan superstition or its moral confusions. Furthermore, a Christian idea of education will be distinguished by a positive appreciation of everyday life and economic work. It will not, in idealistic snobbery, ignore the fact that man has a stomach and must eat, and that he is created with sexual desires. It will not forget, in these spheres particularly, that man is both God's creation and a sinner. It will not therefore discard the wealth of new knowledge which modern biology has given us, but it will refuse to accept pseudo-scientific mythology without fearing the reproach of backwardness. It will not refuse to see man as a member of the animal realm, but will at the same time emphasise that his humanity is something perfectly new which cannot be derived from animal life. It will, however, interpret this humanity of man not so much in terms of his rational and creative capacities as in terms of personality, and will therefore subordinate both his natural and cultural requirements to his ultimate personal destiny. It will put love and personal responsibility in the first place and thus oppose the intellectualism and irresponsible individualism and aestheticism of modern higher education, which is so largely responsible for the cultural catastrophe of our age. In an age of collectivist totalitarianism, Christian education is particularly called upon to oppose the claims coming from that side and to emphasise the supreme value of personality and personal responsibility.

These are merely a few hints indicating that there is a Christian idea of education although we may not yet clearly know what it is. Those who feel the calling to work it out will have to justify their claim to do so by making use of the most important beginnings—the contributions of Pestalozzi and Kierkegaard—and by seeing clearly the real crux of the problem: the relation between *traditio*—Christian and otherwise—and Socratic self-development.

V
WORK

MEN do not work as a matter of course; still less do they want to work when they are not forced by necessity. Is working something essentially human, or is it alien to the human as such, and merely imposed upon men by outward necessity? There are societies belonging to primitive civilisation—notably the Australian aborigines—in which men do not work. They merely catch fish and gather berries when they are hungry. There is, on the other hand, a state of highly developed civilisation in which the bearers of cultural tradition think it unworthy to work. The intensity of work in modern western civilisation is a historical anomaly. Perhaps the weakening of the will-to-work which we experience in some parts of Europe is a reaction against this anomalous tempo of work. At any rate it is a symptom of the unsolved problem of the meaning of work.

If you ask, "Why does man work?" the answer is generally: "Because unless he works he goes hungry. If this necessity ceases, he stops working and plays." This answer is obviously only part of the truth. There are people who want to work, who do not feel at their ease without working, or for whom work is an obligation of self-respect. They would feel themselves to be idlers, parasites of human society if they did not take part in work, which is the basis of existence for civilised humanity. There are people to whom work is a religious obligation, a divine calling. The problem of the meaning of work leads us right into the ultimate question of the meaning of life itself.

Few people philosophise about their jobs. One *does* work, and anyone who doesn't want to will soon see that he has to. For most people the question does not arise, because there is no alternative; that is why history often leaves us without a definite answer. Most men work because they must; whether this is their only motive or whether, apart from necessity, there are other stimuli, remains an open question. But the question takes on specific urgency when under certain social conditions the necessity to work has been somehow loosened or even removed. It is because of this close connection with outward necessity that work is suspected of being a mere servitude of human existence, a burden which must be thrown off by those who have a higher idea of life.

This was the view of classical antiquity. To work for the necessities of life is something degrading for men. Work is good for what the Greek called *banausoi*—the Helots and slaves—not for the free Hellenes. The Greek free man should be exempt from this necessity: he, the bearer of spirit, shall lead a spiritual existence. Certainly, he should not be inactive; activity belongs to the essence of the mind and therefore to a truly human existence. But this activity should not be work, it should not have anything to do with preservation of physical life. The free man ought to create, but he ought not to work. This accords with the Greek philosophical anthropology, namely, that the distinctive element of the human is the spirit, while the body is the *partie honteuse* of man's existence. Therefore free spiritual activity, grounded in itself and not tied to any biological necessity, is the only worthy existence for man. Useful work aimed at preserving life is a mere continuation of animal existence; biological necessity is the lowest category of human purpose, making the mind an instrument of animal instincts.

This depreciation of useful work has never been expressed more clearly or rationally than by Aristotle. But in this, as in so many other respects, Aristotle is a true spokesman of typical Hellenic views. Along with the Aristotelian theory of values, this conception of work was introduced into the Christian Middle Ages and blended with the feudal class structure of society. Only it was no longer spiritual activity in the cultural, but in the religious sense, which forms the apex of this structure. The lowest class is that of the peasant, his activity being the continuation of animal life; the highest is that of the *homo religiosus;* between the two extremes there is a scale determined by the Aristotelian classical opposition of spirit and matter.

This order of values broadly determines the views of the cultured European. He distinguishes between " low " work and " higher " (cultural) activities of man. Economic activity, manual work, is " low ", whilst free, creative, cultural activity is " high ". And it is so much the higher as it is independent of the shameful link with the necessities of life. The highest spiritual activity therefore is that of the free artist or scholar who has not—or should not have—to worry about his living.

This Aristotelian scale of values, which for centuries has dominated European civilisation, has not remained unchallenged. It was in the middle of last century that a radical reaction took place in Karl Marx's economic theory of history. The devaluation of useful economic work gave way to its opposite, which we might call " the myth of the working man ". Economic work to produce the necessaries of life now becomes the real substance of human history and of man's life; according to Marx this is the theme of all history. And the dramatic factor is merely the distribution of the fruit of this work. Let us not forget that the Greek devaluation of economic work was possible only on the basis of slavery. Whilst the Athenian gentlemen were philosophising in the market place, their slaves had to do the drudgery under inhuman conditions, as beasts of burden, so that the Athenian gentlemen, having gained an appetite from their philosophical disputes, might have something worth while to eat on coming home. Similarly the aristocratic-clerical class-system of the Middle Ages was possible only on the basis of agricultural serfdom, the thrall having to do the mean, low work for the higher and the highest ranks, the nobility and the clerical aristocracy. It is in view of these facts that the Marxian picture and its protest against hypocritical ideology and fictions gain their power of conviction. All this cultural existence, it was said, was based upon exploitation. At the cost of the drudgery of the peasant, the higher classes could lead their parasitic, spiritual luxury-existence. Idealism, according to Marx, solves the problem of the meaning of work by dividing it into two parts—spiritual activity and economic work; acknowledging only the first as human, but at the same time living upon those who by necessity do the second. This idealistic conception, then, is characterised by an insincere dualism. It asserts the possibility of a spiritual life without economic interests, whereas the spiritual life can only be lived because the economic necessities are provided by others who are stupid or powerless enough to do it.

I do not hesitate to give a large measure of credit to this Marxian "debunking" of a false, dualistic conception of work. By this Marxian reaction the worker—now the labourer—becomes the "real man". The one who, according to the Aristotelian and the medieval theories was the lowest, the producer of economic values, now becomes the true bearer of human history and civilisation. The working man is the hero of the social revolution and its eschatology. He is the centre of the new myth and the content of the new religion.

This radical turn, however, would not have been possible without a thorough preparation in the bourgeois mentality and society. In a way, Marxism is only a last phase of bourgeois capitalism. It was then that the transvaluation of values from the spiritual to the material economic scale of values took place. That economic values are the highest, the genuine reality, is not an invention of Karl Marx, but of capitalist society of the 19th century. This pan-economism was practically the philosophy of the time, long before Karl Marx gave it the theoretical form of "historical materialism". "Money rules the world." The dispute between Marx and the capitalists is merely concerned with the question who shall have money. The view they hold in common is that economic goods are the substance of life. Therefore they agree that the question why we should work cannot arise. Life consists of these two things: making money by producing material goods and consuming them.

This revolutionary transvaluation of the Aristotelian scale of values, by which the lowest becomes the highest, means the self-sufficiency of the economic motive of work: one works, of course, in order to live, and life means enjoying the goods produced. While the classical solution is based on a fictitious idealism—fictitious because it presupposes the very unidealistic separation of society into a cultural élite and a majority of uncultural, unfree economic producers—19th century economics, both capitalist and Marxist, represents a practical materialism in which man's life and economy are ultimately identical. The first solution corresponds to an anthropology in which man is essentially spirit, imprisoned in a body. The second, materialist, solution corresponds to an anthropology in which man is essentially a body, and mind or spirit merely a concomitant by-product of the body, producing in its turn the so-called ideologies. Both solutions are equally unsatisfactory and unrealistic.

Christian anthropology avoids the idealistic as well as the materialistic onesidedness. It takes man to be a unity of body and mind, because the body is created by God as well as the spirit. The classical hierarchy of values, calling the bodily life "low", is impossible here. Therefore bodily work is in no way degrading, unworthy of men. Instead of the opposition between the "low" and the "high", we find here the relation of ends and means, of "within" and "without". The body is the organ and the means of expression of man's divine destiny. Man must not be ashamed of his body and its needs, both being created by God and therefore good. Work done by the body and for the body is not inferior, but a consequence of God's will. The Bible does not show any trace of an ascetic devaluation of bodily and economic life. The medieval predilection for virginity and for a religious life detached from the world has its roots not so much in Christianity as in Hellenistic antiquity.

Luther's rediscovery of the Biblical meaning of " vocation " or " calling " had revolutionary consequences. In the Middle Ages it was only the monk and the priest who had a divine vocation, not the layman. The idea of the *homo religiosus* being, by his divine vocation, the apex of the social scale dominated the whole of the structure of feudal society, culminating in the Pope and—at the other extreme—the peasant in an almost slave-like abasement. He, of course, had no divine vocation; this was the exclusive privilege of the *homines religiosi.* It was a direct consequence of Luther's rediscovery of the New Testament message that every Christian, whether a priest, a monk, a king or a housemaid, being called into the service of God, may look at the work he or she is doing as a divine calling or vocation. There is nothing " low " about the work of a housemaid. It is just as " high " as reading the mass or the breviary. It does not matter what you do, provided that whatever you do is done as a divine service to the glory of God.

By this new idea of calling or vocation the fatal dilemma is removed: the choice is between the highest valuation of the spiritual with a consequent devaluation of the economic physical work, or the removal of this dualism on the basis of a merely materialistic economy. If all work is divine service, it is ennobled by this highest calling. The difference in value no longer lies in the kind of work which is done, but simply in its having, or not having, this divine purpose. The housemaid, the peasant, the cobbler, the industrial worker have equal title to divine nobility as the judge, the abbot, the artist or the king, if they do their work as a divine " calling " or vocation. The valuation of work is shifted from the " what " to the " why " and " how ".

This new conception of vocation therefore ennobles the common man and his working day. Wherever a labourer does his work as God's servant, he has a better claim to a spiritual existence than an artist or scientist who knows nothing of divine calling. The traditional conception of spiritual work proves to be false. Spiritual work is done wherever work has this highest perspective. Our traditional conception of spiritual work originates from that abstract idealism which separates spirit and body. This spiritual snobbery is the counterpart of materialist vulgarism. Both are overcome by a truly Christian understanding of vocation. This high valuation of economic work as being a service of God cannot fall a prey to materialistic vulgarisation any more; the valuation of intellectual or aesthetic work as being a service of God, no more and no less than the work of the farm-labourer seen in the same perspective, leaves no room for spiritual snobbery. The farmer, Johannes, in Gotthelf's *Uli, der Knecht,* who sits at night with his servant, Uli, to watch a calving cow, and uses this time to talk to him about his problems as a Christian brother, is enjoying a spiritual existence just as much as Johann Sebastian Bach composing a cantata in honour of God.

Work conceived as the service of God is at the same time serving men. On this basis the division of labour cannot lead to the formation of classes or castes. Employer and employee, government and people, are brothers. If people take their Christian faith seriously, everyone knows that his specific function in society is service for the common good. Higher power, as involved in higher office, means so much greater responsibility for service. The Christian conception of vocation does not remove functional hierarchy. There is an Above and a Below, there is graded competence. But all this is functional, *dienstlich,* as we say in German—a term which refers to service, and has nothing whatever to do with distinction of value, nor any connotation of unfreedom. The soldier has to obey the officer, but the officer is not " more " than the soldier. In spite of functional subordination, they are equal.

Karl Marx saw clearly that the division of labour, as it has developed in history, is closely related to the development of different kinds of feudalism, of caste and class systems in which the so-called " higher " exploits the so-called " lower ". He saw, further, that all sorts of metaphysical and religious ideas have been used to justify these systems of exploitation. It is hardly his fault that he did not see the true social consequences of the Christian idea of vocation, because empirical Christianity did not manifest much of it. It is within the so-called Christian world that the feudal structure of the Middle Ages and the class structure of modern society originated. Just as in classical antiquity society shows a cleavage between an unfree majority doing the economic drudgery and a free non-working *élite* forming the basis of a cultural life, so in the age of capitalism there was a cleavage between those living on independent capital income and those living on dependent wages. Because capital income is independent, while wage-income is dependent, the capitalist can decide how the proceeds of the work are to be divided, which, of course, he does entirely for his own profit. To oversimplify grossly: he takes the gold for himself, gives silver to the management, and the copper to the worker. In this fashion a modern caste system is formed within a society with equal political rights. There is a small *élite* having the means of a rich cultural existence, while the larger masses are doomed to cultural helotism. The non-working *élite* lives at the cost of the hardworking mass, on the backs of which it produces and consumes the higher cultural goods.

Onesided as this analysis may be, there is so much obvious truth in it that the masses of the working people, having once become aware of these facts—at the same time being misled by the onesidedness and exaggerations of this theory of exploitation—cannot have a right attitude to their work. This is one of the main causes of the present crisis of labour. The second cause seems to be of a merely technical nature, but is closely related to the first: the progressive division of labour, with its ultimate development, the assembly-line method of production.

Once the owner of capital is separated from the actual work, his only motive is profit. In order to increase profit, he has to accelerate the process of work to get as much out of his invested capital as possible. The human factor, the relation of the workers to their work, is of secondary, if any, importance. More and more the machine thinks for the worker, while the share of the individual worker in the meaningful whole of the work decreases. The relation of the worker to his work becomes more and more impersonal and the meaning of his work becomes invisible. He seems to be merely an unimportant part of the machinery, whilst the meaning of what he does passes from his horizon. Much of the satisfaction felt by the farmer, in his intimate relation to natural growth, and the artisan in creating a useful object, is denied the worker at the assembly-line.

The third cause of the crisis may be more important than the two others: unemployment and insecurity. The deep-rooted fear of unemployment shows more clearly than anything else that man does not work merely in order to get his living. Unemployment is dreaded even where its economic effects are minimised by insurance. Why then is unemployment so greatly feared? First, because it throws a man out not merely of a job, but of meaningful work which gives his life the dignity of creativity and service. Second, because it gives the unemployed the feeling of being a parasite of society. He feels himself, although innocently, under sentence of the judgment, " If any will not work neither let him eat ". He feels he is living at the cost of other people. He is ashamed to eat what others produce. It is this fear of unemployment, inherent in our present economic system, which more than anything else makes him hate this system and his working share in it. It is this permanent insecurity of the wage-earner which makes him conscious of his dependence and his social rootlessness.

It cannot be denied that these are features of our prevalent western economic system. It is another question whether a collectivist state-socialist system would make much difference to the worker's attitude to his work. A nationalised economy will not stop the progressive division of labour, nor abolish the assembly-line. The nationalisation of capital will not remove the dependence of the individual worker. Whether a state-controlled economy will be able to avert unemployment is at least an open question. On the other hand, it cannot be doubted —because it is already proved—that collectivism creates new factors which are unfavourable to a positive valuation of work. In a complete state-economy, the worker would hardly be allowed to strike or to choose his own working place, while he would always have to fear the punishment of an omnipotent employer.

It is one of the main effects of a truly Christian view of life that one does not accept the alternative of capitalism or collectivist state-economy. This " either-or " is a false abstraction, disproved by history. Pure capitalism, as seen by Marx, does not exist any longer, because of the powerful reaction of trade unionism and state legislation. We are, however, far from having exhausted all the economic reserves of a conception of work which is neither individualistic nor collectivist, based neither on a false idealism nor on a false materialism, but upon a Christian understanding of man and work.

The attitude to work is ultimately a religious question. Experience shows that even within the present economic system it is not impossible—though it is difficult—to do one's work as service for God and men. If we keep in mind what St. Paul could expect from the slave members of the Christian community, we may come to the conclusion that the primary factor in the crisis of work is the disappearance of the Christian faith. While it is true that all kinds of slavery are a disgrace to a Christian society and have to be fought, it is also true, and even more true, that a real believer can do his work as a service for God and men whatever the system may be. Capitalism in the Marxian sense is just as little reconcilable with Christianity as is totalitarianism. Both have to be fought equally as destructive of the dignity of work. But while it is a serious obligation of the Christian Church to overcome this fatal "either-or", it is the blessing of vital Christian faith to preserve the conception of divine calling even in the most unworthy conditions.

By the Christian idea of vocation all work is personalised as well as communalised. It is seen as part of one social body, as a contribution within a working community. Everyone does his service in his place and within its limits, and therefore gets his appropriate remuneration. The more this communal spirit is alive, the less need is there of the stimulus of privileges for specific services. From this ideal picture of a Christian community, we can deduce the nature of those factors which threaten and destroy the community of work.

First among these is the oligarchic misuse of the functional hierarchy, i.e. the exploitation of the functional subordinates in the interests of a selfish plutocracy or a tyrannical bureaucracy. Whether it is the capitalist "boss" or the communist commissar that is exploiting his functional position for selfish ends makes little difference. By this selfish exploitation of a position of power they make it difficult, if not impossible, for the worker to look at his work as a service. The second danger is ochlocratic, i.e. the fanaticism of equality which has no use for any kind of subordination. Nothing is more ruinous to the community of work than this egalitarianism. It destroys co-operation even more radically than does oligarchic misuse. The mere idea of radical equality poisons the atmosphere of work. Where the feeling is prevalent that any kind of inequality is as such an injustice, there can never be a positive valuation of work until every thing is equalised. This perhaps is the most serious element in the crisis of labour at the present time.

Someone may object that of course division of labour and functional differentiation of competence must exist, but that no kind of privilege should be derived from it. Every servant of the community ought to be treated with absolute equality. Our reply is, first, that wherever this view of equality prevails, even functional differentiation will always be looked at with resentment and jealousy. Radical egalitarianism cannot stand any subordination. Secondly, as human nature is, it is impossible to get functional differentiation without the stimulus of privilege. Only in a society of perfect saints would it be possible to get a maximum of service and the necessary minimum of functional differentiation, with its different degrees of responsibility, without some kind of social privilege as a stimulus. Society has to pay for higher service the price of social privileges.

To ignore this fundamental social law means to ruin any kind of social order. Even Bolshevist society had to learn that. But this fundamental law is discredited wherever the principle of egalitarianism dominates people's minds. It is beautiful if individual Christians, of their own accord, renounce all privilege —examples are not too frequent!—but it is entirely false to make this a general principle of Christian ethics and to discredit privilege in any sense as unethical. Wherever this radical egalitarianism takes hold of people's minds, its levelling results do not stop short of the dissolution of the social order. Equality is a principle of the highest importance within Christian ethics, but radical egalitarianism is the most dangerous poison within any working community. No society and no positive valuation of work is possible where this egalitarianism prevails. In saying this we do not favour unjust inequality, but we wish to discredit the identification of justice with equality.

Apart from egoistic motives, it is only the belief in God's creation which affords a real motive for work. By it man knows two things: that being a spiritual-bodily unity, he is destined to work; and that by being created as a person in community, he is created for community in work. Wherever this faith prevails, the motive of work is guaranteed even in the most unsatisfactory conditions.

Where there is at present a weakening of the will-to-work it is an outgrowth of our artificial civilisation and, at bottom, a consequence of secularism. As we have seen in our lecture on technics, Western society has not proved capable of mastering the technical development in such a way that technical progress could be made serviceable to the human person and to the life of the community. Futhermore, technical " progress " in combination with other factors has led to economic conditions—of which we shall speak in a later lecture—which make it difficult to keep the Christian conception of work. A worker who feels himself exploited by the capitalist can hardly be expected to think of his work in terms of divine " calling ". But let us not forget that these economic conditions, as well as that false autonomous development, are themselves the consequences of a deep spiritual disorientation. Neither the crazy technical development, with its complete disregard for man and its mania of production for the sake of production and profit, nor the " capitalist system ", with its disregard for human personality and community, could have originated in a truly Christian civilisation. In addition, the weakening of the will-to-work is due in no small degree to a false, abstract doctrine of equality derived not from a Christian but from a rationalist idea of man and to a Socialist or Communist utopianism which makes believe that in a completely socialised economy all problems would be solved.

It is also true that modern technics, with its extreme specialisation, has made it hard even for good Christians to look on factory work as a divine vocation. We should not, however, overemphasise *this* element of the present situation. Difficulties arising from technical specialisation are not comparable in gravity with the others. They can be overcome by creative efforts on the part of labour and management. Such efforts are already being made and extensive study is going on with promising results. The Christian community has a specific task in just this field, namely, to work out a concrete doctrine of vocation through its lay members who know the jobs and their threat to working morale, and to demand and to create such technical and psychological conditions as are necessary to regain the lost sense of work as a divine calling.

On the other hand, it is necessary to reshape the social structure of the worker's world in such a way as to take away his feeling of being a mere cog in an impersonal machinery, exploited by impersonal forces. It will be part of this programme to dispel the great illusion of our day that the nationalisation or socialisation of industry would do away with impersonalism and exploitation. But, while all this is true, we should not lose sight of the fact that the main problem is neither technical nor social, but spiritual. So long as the process of secularisation goes on as it has been doing now for two or three centuries, I see no hope whatever of regaining a right atmosphere of work. Whether or not we achieve a reasonable compromise between Capitalism and Socialism, the problem of the motive of work will continue to exist even if suppressed by compulsion. A true solution can only come through a return to that conception of work which the gospel alone can give— the conception that work, whatever it may be, is the service of God and of the community and therefore the expression of man's dignity.

Empirical Christianity has failed to work out this conception of work in an age of technics. It may not be too late to do that still, but it will need no less than a great revival of Christianity in order to make this theory effective on a national and world-wide scale.

To close with, let us have a look at the other possibility: the hypertrophy of the will-to-work, i.e. work-fanaticism. This modern phenomenon is to be interpreted as a spiritual *Mangelkrankheit*.[1] There is a vacuum in the soul, an inner unrest from which one escapes by work. Work-fanaticism is proportional to the poverty of the soul. As nervous people cannot keep still, man with his unrestful soul cannot but work. The modern Western world is somehow possessed with this work-fanaticism as a result of inward impoverishment. Of course there is also another cause of this phenomenon which, however, is closely related to the first, namely, the incessant increase of material claims. But do not let us forget that many who are not inwardly seized by this fanaticism of work suffer all the same from its consequences. Those who do not want to get under the wheels have to adapt themselves to the modern tempo of work. It is fair to say that Western man, from sheer absorption in work, no longer knows what it means to live. You may find even on a tombstone the words: "His life was work". It is here that the fourth commandment comes in: the Sabbath belongs to the order of creation. Man is created by God in such a way that he needs the Sabbath. Where the Sabbath-rest disappears, the human character of life also disappears.

It is a strange paradox of the present day scene that we are suffering from a work-fanaticism and work-idolatry as well as from a lack of will-to-work. This paradox cannot be understood merely by surface-psychology and sociology. Both these phenomena come from the same root, the loss of the sense of the eternal meaning of life. When a man loses this divine perspective, he throws himself into work and becomes a work-fanatic; or he sees no meaning in work and runs away from it, if he is not compelled by necessity or by the state. Just as the true motive of work comes from having a place in God's plan, so the desire of the soul for quiet and true recreation comes from the awareness of a higher destiny. God requires of us both that we do work even if outward necessity does not force us, and that we do rest and give our soul a chance of breathing. It may be that in a near future the problem of leisure will prove just as pressing

[1] Deficiency-disease.

as that of work; indeed it is already becoming one of the major problems of our civilisation. Just as man's work can be emptied of meaning, so can his leisure. The mere escape from work into leisure, and into work from an empty life, is no solution. The real solution is such a conception of life as gives room and meaning to both instead of exchanging one emptiness for another. It has been proved within the Christian community that a life grounded in God's will finds the right rhythm of work and leisure, as expressed in the fourth commandment.

VI
ART

HUMAN activity is not merely working, producing useful things which are necessary for the preservation of life. The human spirit transcends this sphere of vital necessity. Man decorates his home, he adorns his garment and his garden, he builds not only a solid, but a beautiful house, he carves, he draws, he paints without any useful purpose, merely from the inner drive for beauty and self-expression. He makes poetry, he sings, he invents stories, he acts plays. If we ask for a word embracing all that, it seems to be again, as in the case of science, the German language alone which dares to form this all-comprehensive concept of *Kunst,* whilst the English and French, following the Latin tradition, speak of the liberal arts in the plural, including in them also what the German calls *Geisteswissenschaften.* This daring, comprehending conception, which combines the arts of the eye with those of the ear, has the great merit of leading our attention to something common in them all, the element of creativity, which is detached from all usefulness and intent merely upon creating beautiful work for the enjoyment of its beauty.

Many attempts have been made to solve the riddle why men do all this. It cannot be our task to add one more to a hundred existing theories of art, but merely to see how, from the Christian faith, this most mysterious and at the same time most enjoyable phenomenon of culture is to be understood and what its relation is to the Christian faith.

At first sight, art seems to be wholly independent of religion. *Kunst* comes from *können*; a *Künstler* is a man who can do something that others cannot. Similarly we use the word artist, sometimes in a very general sense. We speak of the art of riding, of skating, of tailoring, and so on. But we are conscious that by art in the proper sense we mean something higher. Mere virtuosity is not yet art, although the transition may be gradual. We speak of art in the proper sense where works of permanent value are created. Often art has been defined as the production of the beautiful, and therefore the secret of art has been identified with the secret of beauty. But the idea of beauty seems inadequate to indicate the mystery of art. What has Hamlet or King Lear, what has Goya's " Bull Fight ", what has Strauss' " Eulenspiegel " to do with beauty? Beauty is a fascinating mystery, but art is more mysterious than beauty.

Why do men create works of art? We put aside all accidental motives, such as gaining one's living, love of fame and power. The work of art is so much the greater as these motives are less prominent. Art is surrender to something supra-personal. It originates from an inner urge. It is pledged to a spiritual " ought " which is almost as severe as the moral one; we speak of artistic conscience. We honour Rembrandt who, in his early days a spoilt and prosperous favourite of society, in his later years lost the favour of the public because he painted according to his artistic conscience without any compromise with the taste of the public, so that he died in poverty.

We know that the Aristotelian theory, which gives first place to the imitation of nature, is inadequate, even for the explanation of painting, whilst in all other arts the model of nature hardly plays any rôle. In any case, whether it be in poetry, painting or music, the work of art is the expression of something inward, passing on that inwardness to the one who enjoys it. Art therefore, in all its branches, is expression capable of impressing. But in distinction from speech, it is without direct reference to the " receiver ". It has an objective intention, making it, to a certain degree, independent and indifferent as to whether there is somebody who might enjoy it or not. In medieval glass paintings there are parts which can normally hardly be seen by anybody but which are just as carefully designed and painted as the visible parts. The artistic expression is so united with the inward feeling, that both cannot be detached from each other. The artistic form is externalised inwardness. The true artist does not like to speak of an "idea" of his work, he is—emphatically—not a double of the philosopher. Form and inwardness are one. The artist creating his work creates a second reality distinguished from nature by its anthropomorphism. It is materialised soul and exalted nature. The work of art is the product of imagination. The German word for imagination, *Einbildung*, is an aesthetics in a nutshell. The power of imagination is the capacity to externalise inwardness or to spiritualise matter. Once more we ask: Why do men do this? And why do others enjoy the results? A negative reason is obvious: They want to transcend existing reality because for some reason it does not satisfy. Artistic creation is somehow a correction and completion of reality. The dramas of Shakespeare show us people like ourselves. Why then this duplication of the human tragedy and comedy? The persons of Shakespeare's tragedies are no duplicates of those of every-day experience, they are the products of a sifting enhancement which cuts away what is casual and enlarges the essential. Art is condensation, omitting the unimportant and magnifying the important; art intensifies and elates, it brings order to the chaotic, gives form to the casual and shape to the shapeless, it exalts and ennobles the material reality to which it gives form.

What, for instance, is the meaning of the verse in poetry? If man wants to say something important, he tries to make as great a distance as possible between that and mere talk. He wants to liberate his speech from every-day casualness, he gives it *gebundene Form*. The free submission under a law, the mounting of springing life in a self-chosen discipline, the firm shape of that which otherwise is shapeless, gives his speech lasting form, nobility.

Art, then, is the attempt of man to raise himself out of the casualness, lowness, transitoriness of every-day life to a higher existence. This is the elevating effect of all art whatever its content may be. There is nothing elevating in the content of Othello, but in its form, which gives to human passion a purity, a necessity and an intensity by which it represents a higher form of existence. All art strives with more or less success after perfection which cannot be found in reality. *Art is an imaginary elevation of life in the direction of the perfect.*

Imaginary indeed! Of course a Greek temple or a Gothic cathedral are not imaginary, but very real, built of massive blocks. But the beauty of this work is an imaginary elevation of life, a perfection which does not belong to ordinary existence but stands apart. Art does not change our life. The aesthetic solution of a problem by which a poet gets rid of it is no real solution, no real liberation. Art originates from and lives within imagination; it is an imaginary reality, similar to the dream. As long as we dream happily, happiness is real, but when we awake this happiness is gone. It cannot be integrated into our reality; it stands outside of that continuity which we call reality. Reality is the same to-day and to-morrow, but the dream of to-night will not be the dream of to-morrow. When the sound of Bach's Double Violin Concerto, which filled me with heavenly joy, has faded away, it still somehow remains with me for a while, like a beautiful dream when I awake. But then comes reality which is not heavenly joy, but sorrow and conflict, which the beauty of Bach's Concerto cannot alter.

This is the limit of art. It is imaginary, *playing perfection*. It is the greatness and the delight of art to be perfection; it is its limitation to be merely imaginary perfection. It is the danger of art that it is so powerful although imaginary. Is there really a danger in art? Is art not that one thing in our life for which we can be thankful and which we can enjoy without reserve? This indeed is our first response: as Christians we say: art is one of the great gifts of God the Creator. Works of art are not produced as a matter of course. Talent or genius is the decisive element, and this is a gift of the Creator. It is not in vain that the word "talent" is taken from the Biblical parable which speaks of trusteeship. What then is its danger? It lies close to its very essence. Its essence is to be imaginary, its danger is that imaginary perfection may be confounded with real perfection. Art then becomes a substitute for religion. One looks for something in art, which it is not able to give: real elevation, real perfection. This confusion is what we call aestheticism. Art is not to be blamed for it, and it can be said that the great artists have rarely become victims of this temptation. This confusion of imagination with reality happens more often to those who enjoy art than to the productive genius.

Furthermore, it must be said that art does not really displace religion, but rather fills a vacuum in the soul which ought to be filled by faith. But we cannot evade the question whether there is not a fundamental opposition between art and faith, as expressed in the second commandment of the Decalogue. "Thou shalt not make unto Thee a graven image, nor the likeness of anything that is in heaven above, or that is in the earth beneath, or that is in the water under the earth." Can the believer in face of this unambiguous prohibition enjoy art without reserve? One might reply that the divine prohibition is not referred to art as such but to idolatry, that is, to pantheistic confusion of Creator and creation. The question, however, remains whether art as the work of imagination and as imaginary perfection does not involve a fundamental conflict with faith in the invisible perfect One from whom alone comes real perfection. Is there not a secret opposition between the enjoyment of heavenly beauty in the imaginary world of art and the hope in the real heavenly redemption? Is not art, at its best, some kind of parallel to pantheistic mysticism, both being an anticipation of heavenly bliss here and now?

It seems to me, we must not be extreme on either side. The true artist is no ecstatic who forgets about reality. Great art has always been rather tragic than happy, just as we can say that tragedy is the highest form of art. In tragedy and in all tragic art, man is conscious of his predicament and of his need for redemption. It is only the artist of the second rank who wants to deceive men and himself with the belief that art itself can solve the contradictions of human reality. One great poet, defining the origin and essence of his art, says: *und wo der Mensch in seiner Qual verstummt, gab mir ein Gott zu sagen, was ich leide.* We need not therefore take too seriously that mystical or pantheistic danger, great as it may be, but we must take account of the opposite possibility that art can, by its capacity to intensify and to emphasise the essential, show to man with particular impressiveness his real situation as a creature needing redemption.

We have to face the problem of Christian art. First of all, Christian art is not merely a possibility, but a historical reality. Since the decay of the Roman Empire during more than a thousand years, European art has been "Christian". At first, this does not mean more than that the majority of the works of architecture in this era were Christian churches, from the Byzantine basilicas of Ravenna and Monreale to St. Peter's in Rome and the baroque churches of Germany and Austria. It means, furthermore, that the sculpture of these centuries is primarily Church decoration, that the subject-matter of painting, too, is drawn mostly from Biblical stories of Christian legends, that poetry and music, up to the time of Bach, are dedicated to the service of Church life. It is, then, an indubitable fact—although a fact which needs interpretation—that during more than ten centuries art in all its aspects was an expression primarily Christian in essence and served the Christian Church. The question remains, however, in what sense we can speak of Christian art.

We should beware from the outset of two extreme views: the one is a naïve confusion of Christian art with art, the contents of which or the themes of which are Christian. When certain painters of the 16th century Renaissance treat Biblical themes or Christian legend, it is obvious that this connection between Art and Christianity is merely an outward and casual one. Sometimes, as in the case of the great Peter Breughel, one might even call this relation ironical. Even if we allow for the fact that the religious expression of an Italian is, in any case, more declamatory and dramatic than that of a North European, and even if we grant that Roman Catholic Christianity in itself is more externalised than Protestant, still we must confess that there is a kind of Renaissance art which, in spite of its Christian content, cannot really be called Christian. On the other hand, we cannot acknowledge the formalist theory that it is of no importance for art to have a Christian content or indeed any content at all. Here, then, we are up against the difficult problem of form and content in art.

First, it cannot be denied that in art form and not content is primary. It is great art, when van Gogh paints a sunflower, when Daumier paints a boulevard scene. It is not great art when Kaulbach, in an enormous picture, interprets the Reformation. One might say, then, that content is nothing and form everything. Futhermore, what should " content " mean in pure music? But, on the other hand, could you seriously contend that it does not matter whether Michelangelo chooses as his object the Biblical story of Creation and the Fall or treats some scene of every-day life? Do you think that Bach could express his deepest feelings, as in his B Minor Mass, just as well by using some banal worldly text? Or that it was by chance that Rembrandt in his later years turned more and more exclusively to Biblical stories? What, after all, is form and content when an inward world has to be visibly or audibly incarnated? The relation between art and religion, between art and Christian faith, cannot be accidental, even though there exists supreme art without any noticeable relation to religion. There must be some deep connection between art and religion and, in particular, between art and Christian faith. What is it?

Let us start with Greek tragedy. It may not be of decisive importance that the Greek theatre grew out of a religious ceremony, just as the great manifestation of Greek architecture and sculpture originated from religious life. But tragedy as such—the phenomenon of the tragic—cannot be understood without man's relation to the moral order of the world. Without tragic guilt, no tragedy. It is not by chance that a Christian tragedy does not exist. Not because there was not enough dramatic talent to form a tragedy, but because Christian faith and the tragic understanding of life are irreconcilable. This form of art then, tragedy, has a definitely religious but certainly no Christian basis. How could you separate here form and content? Take a parallel from within Christian times: the Biblical oratorio and the musical Mass, where the text supplies incomparable musical possibilities. Certainly, there do exist oratoria of an entirely secular character; the musical form of an oratorio is not necessarily tied to the Christian content. But it cannot be a matter of chance that so many of the greatest works of music are those in which Christian texts are interpreted by music.

Even if we understand musical art merely from the point of view of dynamic expression, we would still have to take account of the fact that there are emotions of the soul, tensions and contrasts, and therefore a dynamism which cannot be found apart from religious, nay, even Christian faith. If you think of the "Sanctus" or the "Kyrie eleison" of Bach's Mass, you can hardly deny that such music could not be created but by a deeply Christian composer. Take another example: It is hardly to be denied that the Roman Catholic faith has a closer relation to the arts of the eye than the Protestant, that, on the other hand, Protestant church music has reached heights which no Catholic composition has attained to. Roman Catholic faith tends to the visual, its relation to the visible is essentially positive, whilst Evangelical faith clings to the Word and has only an indirect and uncertain relation to the visible. That is why painting disappears in the Protestant Church, whilst church music acquires an importance which it never had before.

The relation between art and religion, art and Biblical faith, must not be studied merely to answer the question as to what importance the religious element has for art; but also from the other viewpoint, to answer the question whether religion and Christian faith do not in themselves tend towards artistic expression. The Christian community through the ages has been a singing community. Christian worship is hardly thinkable without a hymn, psalm, chorale or anthem. The praise of God, joyful thanks, and passionate supplication of the congregation almost necessarily take shape in singing. There is hardly a more alarming, though infallible criterion of the decline of Christian community life than the decadence of Christian church music in the last two centuries. The Christian hymns that have been invented and sung during the last century have little to do with art, whilst the choral melodies which abounded in the first two centuries of the Reformation churches were works of art of the first order; even Bach, who did not himself produce one, showed almost envious admiration of them.

Not every live Christian is *ipso facto* also a church musician, but where musical talent comes within the life-stream of faith and within the magnetic field of a true Christian community, church music is born inevitably. The same can be said with regard to the relation of faith and poetic form. All the great prophets of Israel, from Amos to the anonymous writer of the exile, were also great poets. The weakening of poetic power goes hand in hand with the weakening of prophetic originality in the later Old Testament prophets. There is hardly a word of Jesus which is not a little poem and some of His parables are poetry of the highest order. We can hardly imagine Luther's prophetic genius apart from the powerful rhythm of his hymn, " A mighty fortress is our God ". That is Luther! Who is able to delimit here prophetic faith and poetic expression? Both are so united in this hymn that the power of faith and the power of expression cannot be distinguished.

A similar relation is to be observed conversely: in respect of *im*pression. The religious hymn is not merely a necessary expression of faith, but also an effective means of faith. It is as if sacred music " tuned the soul " for faith. As the Marseillaise was a powerful factor in spreading the spirit of the French Revolution, in a similar way really Christian music can kindle faith. The music of Bach and Schütz has this effect, but not that of Wagner. There are works of Bach to which, though they are pure music without any text, one could add the adequate Biblical words. We know by now that his most abstract composition, *Die Kunst der Fuge,* is Christian theology expressed in the form of immensely complicated fugues.

Something similar is a common experience in the sphere of architecture. A Gothic cathedral generates a certain kind of reverent feeling, without there being any direct indications of the cultus. The very structure of the Gothic church, being an expression of medieval religion and theology, impresses the mind with that same spirit from which it originates. It is utterly inept to build a modern bank in Gothic style. If the so-called Gothic civil architecture of the Middle Ages does not have this character of dissonance, it is because in that era all life was permeated by the spirit of its theology and piety. How far, however, this Gothic structure is Christian, and how far neoplatonic mysticism is its root, is another question.

If then there exists an indubitable relation between faith and art on the side of expression as well as on that of impression, we cannot avoid the question what the fate of art will be in a thoroughly secularised society where faith has ceased to be a formative factor. Indeed, this question is not merely academic in our time. It would not be historically correct to claim, on the basis of what has been said before, that the decline of religion must necessarily carry with it the decay of art. History gives many clear examples to the contrary. Greek art reached its zenith at a time when religion had already begun to decay. The same is true of Renaissance art in the 16th century, and French painting was at its best in the age where positivist and even materialist philosophy dominated. Again, a similar observation can be made about German music from the time of Mozart onwards, the only exception, confirming the rule, being Bruckner. And if instead of speaking of epochs we think in terms of individual artists, it would be hard to discover any definite proportion between artistic power and perfection on the one hand, and religious intensity on the other. Alongside Michelangelo and Fra Angelico, we have Raphael, Leonardo and Titian; alongside Rembrandt, we have Peter Breughel and Vermeer; alongside Bach, we have Gluck and Strauss, not to speak of certain schools of first-rate art with a decidedly frivolous conception of life as background.

Let us remember once more that *Kunst* comes from *können*, that artistic genius is a natural disposition, and as such indifferent to religion or any philosophy of life. Whether a man who is born with creative genius is deeply religious or indifferent to religion, does not in itself increase or diminish his creative capacity. But in spite of this we venture to contend that in a society where religious faith is dead, or has been dead for a while, art also decays. It is difficult to prove this assertion from history, because, whilst there have been times of religious decline, there never has been an epoch of predominant atheism. There may be one exception to this rule: our own age, as far as certain countries are concerned. But this period has not yet lasted long enough for us to draw definite conclusions. All the same our assertion does not hang in the air, for there are strong reasons for its validity.

Whilst it cannot be said that faith or religious power is a necessary presupposition of art, two statements can hardly be denied. First, that creative genius combined with religious depth produces ultimate artistic possibilities which otherwise do not exist. Secondly, no artistic life can thrive on dehumanised soil. Where men are no longer capable of deep and great feelings, where the spiritual horizon has lost infinity, where the understanding of life is devoid of all metaphysical or religious depth, art cannot but degenerate to mere virtuosity, and creative originality exhausts itself in inventions which may be witty, striking or pleasant, but which cannot move the depth of the heart. The grand passions, which are the source of all genuine art, are not a phenomenon of merely psychological dynamic. Grand passions are not merely a matter of temperament or instinct. Their greatness originates not from natural dispositions but from spiritual tensions which do not exist any more where thinking clings to the surface of things.

We touched on this point when we spoke about tragedy. Christian faith in itself cannot accept the tragic view; but being in itself the victory over tragedy, it presupposes the understanding of the tragic. Where there is neither understanding of the tragic nor Christian faith, where all relation to something transcendent and absolute has disappeared, where crude naturalism and materialism have taken the place of religion and metaphysics, great passions, deep feelings and those mysterious longings of the soul out of which great art is born, disappear also. The decay of the truly human necessarily brings with it the decay of beauty and mystery. This decay of the truly human, however, cannot be avoided in a materialistic world.

When man is cut off from the third dimension of depth, when he lives on the surface of mere utility, animal instinct and economic rationality, the element of humanity vanishes. This assertion, I think, has been sufficiently proved in the first series of these lectures.

We now are in a position to see the dual fact: art in its dependence on, and its independence of, religion. The dependence is absolute only in an indirect sense, relative and partial in the direct sense. In so far as the depth of human existence is founded ultimately in the "third dimension", in religion and metaphysics, and in so far as the Christian faith produces the deepest and most human kind of existence, art is dependent on it. In so far, however, as in the individual case and for a certain time this deep humanity can exist after the faith which has produced it, has disappeared, like an evening light after sunset, like the marvellous *Abendrot* in our Swiss Alps, art can persist for a certain while in individuals or during a whole generation after the sunset of faith. But this *Abendrot* cannot be of long duration. The stock of human values created in a time of faith is soon exhausted in a time of faithlessness and with it the possibility of real art. The humanity of man is much more historical than we usually think, and that is true of art.

I think we are justified in applying this general observation to our time, although we have to do it with great caution. If what I have just said is correct, we should expect that the secularisation of modern mankind—which, although fortunately not complete, is the characteristic feature of the modern age—must have its effects on art. And we should guess that this effect must be a certain loss of depth and at the same time a tendency in two directions: barbarism or crudeness as a result of the lost distinction between man and animal nature on the one hand, and a certain abstractness as a result of formalism, because of the disappearance of metaphysical and religious content. Now, with all the reserve which my little knowledge of contemporary art puts upon me, I think that these tendencies are indeed quite obvious in the artistic production of our time, although the reaction against them is also to be felt, and in a quite remarkable degree. But this reaction against barbarism and formalism is at the same time also a reaction against secularisation and to this extent proves our thesis.

Let me point out another feature of modern art which is a necessary result of what I called the loss of the third dimension of depth. Where men lose their religious faith, art is apt to take the place of religion. That danger, which as we have just seen is immanent in all art, becomes real. Art itself becomes the highest value, aestheticism becomes the religion of the time. It can hardly be denied that this is true for a good many of our contemporaries. The imaginary perfection and elevation of life which art gives them becomes a substitute for real salvation. They live in their imaginary world of artistic creation as in a sort of earthly heaven or paradise, measuring all life by their art and artistic genius. If I am not wrong, this is one of the elements which account for the sad condition of the French nation. The prevalent aestheticism of French cultural life has broken or at least seriously damaged its moral backbone. The religion of art is a poor substitute for true religion as a basis of civilisation.

Still, real faith has not vanished. On the contrary, it is just in the sphere of modern art that we find, along with barbarism and formalism, most impressive signs of a spiritual awakening parallel to the reawakening of Christian theology and religious philosophy. Perhaps we may venture to say that the art of our time confirms what we have seen happening in other fields, that the low point of the secularist movement is already passed. At any rate, the battle is on and all of us are engaged in it.

To close—let me take up once more the question raised in the beginning. Why do men create works of art? What is the function of art in the human household? For the creative artist himself this question hardly exists. To him art is a " calling ". To some of the greatest artists it is a divine calling. They follow an inward " must " which permits no further derivation except the religious one. For most men, however, who are not artists, but mere lovers of art, the answer is, from the Christian point of view : art is the noblest form of resting from the struggle of life, closely related with the quiet of the Sabbath in the Biblical sense. All work, even the highest spiritual work, produces a kind of hardness and cramp. The man who knows nothing but work becomes soulless. Art is the noblest means of re-creation. It cannot redeem our soul, but it can "tune the heart", even for the highest: for communion with God. It never produces or creates faith, but it can support the Word of the Gospel, which creates faith. It can open the closed soul and help it to relax in the most human way from the stress of everyday life. That is why we sing in our church services and why we should not underestimate the function of real church music. But apart from this highest function, man needs relaxation, especially if he is engaged in intellectual work. Art is the beneficent mediator between spirit and sensuality. It is a spiritualisation of the sensual and the sensualisation of the spiritual. It is a necessity primarily for those who do not live in immediate contact with nature. Art is therefore, before all, a necessity for the city man. What Luther and Bach have said of music is true of all art: it is the servant of God to help his sorrowful creatures, to give them joy worthy of their destiny.

VII

WEALTH

ALL civilisation is built upon material goods. So long as man lives "from hand to mouth", so long as there are no permanent material goods and fixed property, civilisation cannot arise. Notwithstanding the moral and social dangers of wealth and the acquisitive instinct, the fact remains that higher civilisation presupposes a certain material wealth and stable conditions of property. One cannot deny that cultural life always has a certain *bourgeois* character. The beginning of civilisation coincides with the transition from nomadic life to agriculture and permanent residence. It is not by mere chance that the word culture originates from agriculture. Agriculture is the primary stage of man's mastery of nature. Agriculture brings with it permanent and communal residence and city-building, which in its turn involves the crafts and division of labour. Division of labour again makes possible barter and its rationalised form, money.

Of course, historically, the first property of man is neither soil nor house nor money, but the tamed animal and the weapon. The nomad is proprietor of his herds; this property is, so to say, entirely natural. The struggle between mine and thine, the problem of property, becomes acute only through the competition for soil and particularly because of individual agricultural property. On the other hand, the development of individual personality seems to be closely related to individual property. Where the peasant works a field that does not belong to him, where he is not economically independent, he will hardly become morally free. It is a law deeply rooted in man's nature that man ought to be free to dispose of the produce of his work, that its fruit " belongs " to him. Wherever this law has been disregarded, as in the absentee-proprietorship of the

Roman Empire, this has been a cause of cultural decline. Individual property is an important ethical value. We should not forget, however, that what nowadays is called individual property is of a very different nature. Modern individualism has transformed the firm relation between man and "his" soil into its very opposite, making agricultural soil an object of capitalist speculation.

A similar relation to that which exists between man and soil obtains also between man and his house and his tools. In order to develop as a free personality, man must have certain things that belong to him. It is true that even a slave—like Epictetus—may consider himself a free man, as did the slaves of the New Testament Church, considering themselves as free in Christ. But as a general rule, the connection between individual property and the development of free personality can hardly be denied. A certain economic independence is a prerequisite of free personality. Private, i.e. individual, property is recognised in the Bible as a matter of course, although it is never considered as an absolute right. It is limited by the idea of stewardship under God and by the regard for the common good. The short experiment of Christian communism in the community of Jerusalem does not really form an exception, because everyone was free to place at the disposal of the community whatever he thought fit.

As has already been said, division of work, together with permanent residence, makes possible barter and money. Money is the abstract form of material goods. This abstraction, like all abstraction, includes both great potentialities and great dangers. With money you can buy everything: land, houses, industrial products, and even labour. The economics of money compared with barter may be compared to the relation between algebra and simple arithmetic. Where money has become the main material good, quantity tends to prevail over quality. The desire for wealth becomes infinite. I cannot imagine an infinite number of concrete material goods, but I can easily add an indefinite number of ciphers to any given figure. That is why money becomes a great danger to social life. In itself it is a most valuable invention, freeing the exchange of goods from chance and other limitations and giving economic life a new mobility.

Material property, necessary in itself, becomes deeply problematic through the sinful nature of man, in two respects: first, with regard to the relation of material goods to other values; second, with regard to the relations between men. Let us call the first danger practical materialism. In itself man's desire to acquire property is necessary both for the individual and for society. Cultural life can develop only where a certain surplus of means beyond bare existence is granted. A nation can apply itself to cultural production only where its energies are not entirely occupied by the production of the necessities of life. On the other hand, interest in material property tends to become isolated and monopolistic. Instead of being a *means* of life, wealth becomes the main aim. The necessary acquisitive instinct degenerates into mammonism, money, the abstract form of goods, playing a large part in this dangerous development. The lust for property becomes particularly dangerous when it is combined with the lust for power. Money becomes the primary means of domination over others. And this is the second form of the sinful development of material property. Man wants to be wealthy at the cost of others, and he wants to be wealthy in order to replace social responsibility by domination.

These two negative aspects of material goods are as old as civilisation. Their most primitive forms are theft and robbery; their more refined, but not less pernicious, forms are unscrupulous competition and exploitation, the use of power for material advantage, and the use of money to wield power. The motive of power has two aspects: people may desire material goods in order to get power. or may use power in order to get material goods. All these possibilities are realised even in the most primitive civilisations. They have taken different shapes in the various epochs with their different social, economic and political structures, but basically they are always the same. It is of no small importance to see this *semper idem*, because otherwise one is easily deluded by slogans putting the blame on specific social structures. Whether the economic structure is primarily agricultural or industrial, whether it is characterised by barter, money or credit, whether the political structure is monarchic, aristocratic or democratic, we see always the terrific interplay of man's lust for wealth, ruining his own soul and endangering the life of his fellow men and general culture. On the other hand, the identity of the basic forms should not make us overlook differences arising from the various social, economic or political structures.

We have already seen that money, the abstract material good, accentuates certain evil developments, if not necessarily, at least as a matter of fact. In a similar way we now have to think of certain other factors tending in the same direction. Just as money is an abstract form of barter, credit is an abstract form of money. It is an abstraction of a higher order. In both cases abstraction is in itself a positive factor; it widens out the narrow limits of economic life, set by the more concrete forms of goods. By credit one is enabled to work with the money of others, paying them a certain interest as a reward for lending their money, or giving them shares proportional to one's own gains. This expansion and intensification of economic possibilities at first sight looks quite harmless and useful. But upon closer inspection it carries with it great dangers. It creates income without work on the one hand, and it separates economic production from economic power. The non-working money-giver controls the actual work and the distribution of its profit.

This new economic technique of the modern age, however, reached its full importance only in combination with the transition from craft to machine industry. The tool of the craftsman is cheap and can be owned by anyone. The machine, however, the factory, the industrial plant, is expensive; the individual cannot afford it, he is dependent on credit. Industrialisation is possible only in combination with credit, in its two forms: interest-earning and share-taking credit. Herein originates that system which we call capitalistic, and which at first is a merely technical device that must be sharply distinguished from what we call the "capitalistic spirit". Taken for granted that all the persons concerned are good Christians, free from greed or egoism, this capitalistic system combined with industrialism would work for good. But just as money, the abstract form of goods, brings with it danger, even more does capitalistic credit become morally dangerous as soon as our moral hypothesis ceases to hold. In its combination with egoistic motives, this credit system becomes what is called capitalism in the evil sense of the word. Why is that so?

First, in expanding the possibilities of profit-making, it also intensifies the profit motive. This is the effect of the doubled abstraction. Just as money can be more easily desired in indefinite quantities than concrete goods, profit-bearing securities can be more easily desired indefinitely than money. The pure quantification of the material goods tends to unlimited desire. Second, the development of the capitalist system means the gradual separation of ownership of the tools—machine, factories, etc.—and actual working with those tools. It creates dependent labour and independent capital. It is particularly the absentee-owner, the anonymous shareholder who, not knowing those who actually do the work and their conditions, is free from those moral inhibitions of the profit motive which are likely to function wherever work is done in personal co-operation. Third, the difference in economic power between the dependent workmen and the independent proprietor of the productive capital goes on increasing. Fourth, this economic power, concentrated in a few hands, may become so great that it can influence and perhaps even control political power. Big business is an important factor in world politics.

So far, we have followed the analysis of capitalism given by Karl Marx, which, generally speaking, is correct. But certain corrections in his picture are necessary. Like his teachers of the Manchester school of economics, Karl Marx also presupposes the pure *homo oeconomicus*, taking for granted that the person who has economic power will use it without any consideration for the community or the human individual. This is wrong. The sense of justice and human personality is an important element even in a capitalist society. Second, Karl Marx has not taken account of the fact that through the trade-union movement and state legislation the evil consequences of the capitalist system can be and have been checked to a large extent. Capitalism in Marx's sense, i.e. unlimited exploitation of labour in the exclusive interest of capital profit, hardly exists any more in Western society. All the same, the moral dangers inherent in the capitalist system have become and still are sinister realities: tremendous intensification of the profit motive, increased inequality with regard to property and power, social disintegration. There does exist what Karl Marx calls a "proletariat", i.e. enormous masses of men living under conditions unworthy of and detrimental to human personality, as well as to true community and spiritual cultural life.

The necessary reaction against this threat from above has created what Karl Marx calls the class struggle, which, of course, is not merely a Communist programme, but a double-sided fact, poisoning and disintegrating society. The injustices inherent in and produced by the capitalist system and the proletarian disintegration of society have created a mentality within the world of labour which makes men inclined to listen to the slogans of totalitarian Communism, which in itself is the end of free society and of human culture.

By all these factors the problem of material goods is accentuated in a way unknown to previous ages, unknown particularly to the time of Old and New Testament revelation. In the teaching of the prophets, of Jesus, and of the apostles material goods and property are regarded as natural consequences of man's being a creature. The Bible is not ascetic, either in this or in any other respect. In the Old Testament wealth is not morally discredited: it is a divine gift and a manifestation of God's blessing. But there already we do find a very critical estimate both of acquisition of goods and of property. The prophets in particular passionately denounced the egoistic profit-motive, which makes men forget God and trample upon their neighbours. They are uncompromising in passing judgment upon the mighty and wealthy who use their power to exploit and enslave the powerless. In the New Testament this critical attitude becomes even sharper, and wealth appears almost exclusively as a negative value. It seems almost impossible to be rich without forgetting the poor or without forgetting God. The man who enjoys his wealth without being moved and worried by the sight of poverty cannot be a disciple of Jesus. But even there we do not find a general moral disqualification of wealth or the postulate of poverty. The use which the medieval theology made of Jesus' word to the rich young man is a misunderstanding. There is nothing like a general precept or "counsel" of poverty in the teaching of Jesus. Wealth is not in itself evil, but its temptation is almost irresistible. While in the church of Corinth there are "not *many* wealthy", still there are some, just as among those who followed Jesus there were *some* who had means, without being blamed for it.

It is then very difficult, if not impossible, to gain direct norms from the Bible for present-day problems of economic life, in so far as they are predominantly structural. Attempts have been made to derive from the Bible a general prohibition of interest, and therefore a general opposition to the capitalist system. This interpretation, however, identifies two fundamentally different things: interest in the Old Testament sense, and interest as the basis of the credit system, which is entirely unknown in the Bible. To take interest from money lent to a neighbour who is in need is a different thing from deriving interest from money or credit given to someone who wants to make more money by it. The prohibition of interest by the medieval Church has nothing whatever to do with Biblical teaching.

On the other hand, it is obvious that in the age of technical industry and the credit system the problem of material property and acquisition is fundamentally different from what it was in the time when the farmer, the craftsman and the travelling merchant were the predominant figures of economic life. Material property in the modern sense includes power over the dependent non-proprietor and even power over the state machinery. While power in itself is not morally evil, it becomes evil almost inevitably through the possibility of misusing it.

And this possibility again becomes a fact almost inevitably if we take men as they are. The concentration of power inherent in the credit system is an enormous moral danger, both with regard to the just distribution of goods and with regard to the just distribution of economic responsibility and power.

This danger, however, can be and is checked by two counterforces which tend to create economic as well as political balance, viz., by organised labour and by the equalising interference of the state. Furthermore, it is checked by a third factor which is often under-rated and even ridiculed, i.e. by spontaneous self-limitation of those in whose hand is the main economic power. Whether it is from fear of Communism or of organised labour, or whether it comes from a real sense of justice and humanitarian motives, the so-called capitalists have learned to restrict the use of their power. While, of course, this self-limitation is far from having reached the necessary level, it is certain, on the other hand, that without it things would be much worse. It is here that the Christian Church has its most immediate field of action, because within the Christian faith motive is more important than structure. Economic power is not necessarily used unjustly, and therefore power is not in itself an evil, but a great temptation. Where power is controlled by just and disinterested motives, it does not lead to injustice and exploitation. A truly ethical control of motives, wherever it does take place, is a surer safeguard against injustice and selfish exploitation than any structural, i.e. legal and political, control. The change of the system is only a makeshift for the lacking ethical inhibitions in the use of economic power. Wherever the working man is not influenced by propagandist slogans, he does not resent the so-called capitalistic system, if he is sure that the " boss " is truly concerned about his welfare and led by the sense of justice and loyalty. However, this obvious truth is limited by two facts: first, that even the best-minded employer himself is part of a system which limits his good intentions; second, by the fact that with the development of big business the individual employer more and more disappears. The law of big numbers makes itself felt and gives the moral problem of present-day economy a particularly dark aspect. Because the large majority of capitalists are motivated much more by the profit motive than by justice and goodwill, the capitalist system on the whole has morally bad effects, and would have them much more without the check of trade-unionism and state interference.

That is the reason why so many seek the solution of the problem in a radical change of the system, in Communism or —what is merely another name for the same thing—State Socialism. They think that by such a structural change the injustices connected with the capitalist system would disappear. They postulate the nationalisation of all productive capital, convinced that by this measure exploitation of the powerless would be discarded and a just distribution of national income would be safeguarded. This medicine, however, would prove more dangerous than the sickness which it means to cure. By nationalisation the whole of economy is politicised. Every member of the working community becomes a functionary of the state. It is inevitable that this politicisation of economy would lead to the totalitarian state. Totalitarianism, however, means the end of personal freedom, a soulless mechanical monster, compared with which the evils of capitalism—great as they are —must be called tolerable. It is an illusion that in a socialised state economy exploitation disappears. The truth is that it is shifted from the economic to the political field. The political " commissar " takes the place of the economic " boss ". Political bureaucratic hierarchy takes the place of economic competition. It is a complete misunderstanding of human nature to think that greed and lust for power would disappear in a fully state-socialist society. The temptation to misuse power is nowhere so great as in a totalitarian system, because the state machinery cannot allow opposition or even criticism. In a completely nationalised economy the individual worker loses his freedom to choose his working- and living-place; he becomes a state-slave.

We do well to remember Montesquieu's great discovery, the system of " division of powers " embodying his idea: *le pouvoir arrête le pouvoir*. Apart from the moral motive—which, as a rule, proves to be weak in general—it is the only safeguard of justice. This principle of Montesquieu presupposes a pluralist structure. Thus far the misuse of capitalist power has been checked by trade-unionism and democratic state interference. Both contain reserves which are not yet tapped. There are still great possibilities lying in the mechanisms of collective bargaining and of education for mutual understanding between labour and capital, in the further democratisation of economy, in a revision of the legal status of corporations, and in the moderate equalising function of the state. The alternative, "either capitalism or state socialism", is a product of propaganda, of panic and of inadequate thinking.

As we have already said, from the Christian faith no direct conclusions can be drawn for the solution of these complex and abstract problems. We have to beware of the short cut, the idea that a specific affinity exists between Christian community and communism. Christian communalism is at the opposite extreme from State Communism. It is the expression of spiritual freedom. Nowhere in the Bible do we find the idea that corporate or national property is better than individual property. What we do find is the idea of stewardship and of social responsibility. As we have already said, on the basis of Christianity there cannot be absolute property, but only property regarded as trusteeship under God. This trusteeship includes responsibility for one's neighbour. The question, however, which legal system is the best makeshift for those true ethical motives, is never touched, just as the Bible does not say which form of political government is the best to check the misuse of political power.

Sometimes the abolition of the capitalistic system has been postulated from merely economic motives which are only in an indirect sense morally relevant. The idea was that only state-planned economies can avoid unemployment and economic crises. Certainly unemployment is a dreadful plague of modern society, but it is an obvious error to think that state economy as such would cure that disease. Economic crises could be avoided by compulsory economic world-planning, i.e. by a world state; but even then it is most doubtful whether it would have this beneficial effect. On the contrary, it is highly probable that the clumsy functioning of state machinery would be a cause of permanent economic crises. But even if we take it for granted that nationalisation of industry and complete state control of economics could liberate society from the evil of unemployment, this gain would be bought at too great a price, the loss of economic freedom and, ultimately, of political freedom as well.

Why is it that the idea of Communism or State Socialism has captured the imagination of the working-class to such an extent as is the case in our day? First, because the so-called free economy of the Western world has failed to a large extent to prove its capacity of providing for just distribution of national income and property, and of giving the working-man an adequate share in management. The Christian Church ought to take a large share of responsibility for this tragic failure, having omitted to instruct her lay-members about their responsibility for social justice and having accepted as a matter of course the development of a kind of individualistic economy which, at bottom, was irreconcilable with the Christian conception of personality and community. The Church should not, however, try to prove her repentance by supporting the ideology and programme of State Socialism or Communism, which would necessarily produce a kind of society in which not only freedom, but justice also finds no place. Secondly, the Communist or State-Socialist idea appeals to a mentality which is almost exclusively fixed upon security and has lost the sense of personal freedom. This mentality is the product of secularisation, i.e. of the loss of spiritual values, particularly of the Christian faith in which both personal dignity and communal obligation are deeply rooted.

Thirdly, the Communistic or State-Socialist idea is the logical consequence of an idea of man which identifies justice with equality and has no comprehension whatever of the element of subordination and differentiation which are inseparable from any live social order. This egalitarianism has created a deep resentment against anything which has even the faintest similarity with the family pattern of community. Of course Christianity has failed in supporting a kind of patriarchism and paternalism which, in a technical world, could not but work out in autocracy and economic tyranny. But the Church is supremely right in affirming that the family pattern is the Christian pattern of all social life. What needs to be seen is that the family pattern must be interpreted and worked out in our day in quite new forms, doing justice to the legitimate claim of each member of the family to personal dignity and basic independence.

It is here that the Christian Church has a great task to fulfil. The Christian conception of man stands above the false alternative of individualistic liberalism or capitalism and collectivistic State Socialism or Communism. Christianity is absolutely unique in presenting a conception of man in which true personality and true community are not only firmly connected with one another but, at bottom, identical. Wherever a community is firmly grounded in Christian thinking, neither individualistic capitalism nor collectivist Communism or State-Socialism are possible. The " third way " is inherent in the Christian conception of man itself. That is why Christianity is called upon to lead the way wherever the third way is seen as necessary and wherever, out of economic life itself, new schemes of social order emerge which are neither individualist nor collectivist.

At present collectivism is in the ascendent and individualism is on the wane. Christianity has the historical task of raising her voice against the great dangers for human personality as well as for community implied in the collectivist scheme. It can do so with even more conviction, since it is becoming evident on experimental grounds that this is not a case of striking the right mean between justice and freedom. In the collectivist society the individual worker will get less than he has at present in a society which has long ago ceased to be purely capitalistic, less both in material reward for his work and in political, social and cultural freedom. Collectivism means, before all, enslavement; but it also means poverty. What is encouraging for those who survey the present evolution in the social sphere is the fact that amongst those who used to be Marxian Socialists a deep change is taking place, away from Marxism in its ideological as well as its economic and political programme. There is an obvious convergence of the thought and will of those who are trying to find a truly social liberalism and those who are out for a truly liberal Socialism. And it is certainly not by chance that where this reorientation takes place a new openness of mind towards Christianity becomes apparent.

Up to now we have been speaking of the problems arising from differences of economic power. We have now to turn to the other great problem, that of excessive valuation of material goods as such. It is obvious that the capitalistic structure of economic life has intensified the acquisitive instinct and increased the striving for wealth. This practical materialism, however, is unlikely to be discarded in a nationalised economy. Against the *auri sacra fames,* State Socialism is no medicine. The valuation of material goods is independent of legal structure and depends on the whole conception of life. Greed, lust for property, is the most direct manifestation of worldliness. The man who does not believe in God and eternal life is likely to be more intent upon material goods than the man to whom the word " Seek ye first the kingdom of God " is a reality. Of course it might be objected that many Christians have been misers and profiteers. But let us beware of confusion; the man who is a miser and profiteer is *ipso facto* not a real Christian. This criterion is unmistakable in the New Testament. One might even say it is the first criterion. He to whom God's Kingdom is a reality cannot be a money hunter, and a money hunter cannot take seriously the Kingdom of God. You *cannot* love both God and Mammon. But where faith in God disappears, the vacuum which it leaves has to be filled with something. It need not be money. It may be a high spiritual good. But it may be money, and it is very probable that in most cases it *is* money which fills that vacuum. Spiritual goods are rarely capable of filling the heart when the basis of spirituality, God, has disappeared. Loss of faith usually means that

Mammon becomes God. The practical materialism of the Occident is a direct and provable consequence of secularisation.

We must say in this connection a few words about a famous theory pointing in the opposite direction: Max Weber's thesis about the connection between Calvinism and capitalism, which was accepted and spread widely by Troeltsch and also, though in a modified form, by Tawney. This theory seems to me a very dangerous half-truth. It cannot be doubted that the Calvinist-Puritan conception of the Christian life, according to which the elect has to prove his election by his life, combined with the Calvinist emphasis on self-discipline and self-restraint, has contributed to the formation of capital; more exactly, to an increase of material goods which, not being consumed, were available for the expansion of production. It is obvious that these motives, combined with other factors, created conditions favourable to the development of the capitalistic system. But at the same time these motives were strictly opposed to what is popularly called the capitalistic spirit. The true Calvinists and Puritans were by no means money-grubbers, but energetic business men who regarded themselves as stewards of God, and therefore responsible to the community. It is not Calvinistic faith but, on the contrary, the decline of this faith and progressive secularisation which led to the greediness which one has in mind when speaking in a critical sense about capitalism. The Quakers perhaps afford the best example. By thrift, sober living, hard work, and indubitable honesty they became most successful business men and acquired considerable wealth. They did not, however, succumb to the capitalist spirit, but proved by example that even within a capitalistic structure the relation between labour and capital can be just and humane wherever the power inherent in that system is not abused but used for good.

The capitalistic system, however, did not develop because of men who worked much and saved the fruit of their work, but because world trade and industry demanded the creation of credit. There have always been hardworking and at the same time thrifty people, before Calvinism and outside it. The particular development of the capitalist system in the so-called

Calvinist countries has very little to do with Calvinism, and is primarily due to the fact that these countries afforded the most favourable conditions for world trade and industry, and that they were populated by a type of people which in many other respects proved to be particularly energetic. This view of things is confirmed by the fact that the development of high capitalism took place in an age when the Christian faith, whether Calvinistic or not, was on the wane. It is the combination of the credit system and industrialism, with that mammonist spirit which is the result of secularisation, that created the kind of capitalism of which the Western world should be ashamed. The tiny bit of truth lying in Weber's thesis is almost irrelevant compared with the enormous confusion which it has produced and the great injustice which it has done to Calvinist faith.

The economic problems, i.e. the problems connected with the production and possession of material goods, have become so portentous in our time because the development of world trade, machine industry and the credit system took place in an age when the Western world was beginning to lose its religious basis, and when, therefore, money-making and the possession of money seemed more important than anything else. Furthermore, this development took place within a society in which an individualistic conception of life worked towards the dissolution of community life. It can be easily understood that a society which was about to lose its religious and moral basis was hardly capable of solving the enormous social problems which the industrial revolution and the break-down of the patriarchal system had created. It can hardly be doubted that a truly Christian society could have overcome these difficulties at an earlier stage and would thus have prevented some of the worst features of the present Western civilisation. For it is the Christian faith that contains all the necessary forces of direction and healing which are adequate even to a very dynamic economic life: a strong consciousness of personal responsibility and freedom, the willingness to serve one's fellow man, and the limitation of economic interest by the faith in a higher, eternal life.

VIII

SOCIAL CUSTOM[1] AND LAW

IN primitive society, as well as in antiquity and in the Middle Ages, social custom (*Sitte*) and law can hardly be distinguished. In their conjunction they are the solid order of life in which the individual is embedded; they are the skeleton, the permanent constitution, for the behaviour of the individuals and their mutual relations. Western society to-day is characterised by an enormous decay of social custom and, as a consequence, by an enormous increase of laws. The behaviour of the individual nowadays is only to a very small degree ordered by social custom, but to an increasing degree his freedom is limited by legal prescriptions. The causal relation between the two facts is obvious: where social custom is strong, only a minimum of legal prescription is necessary.

The destruction of social custom in modern times is closely connected with the development of individualism. The individual wants to shape his life as it pleases him or as it seems good to him. He does not want to be controlled by the anonymous power of social custom. He wants to have his liberty, and he also wants to decide according to his own conscience. The decay of social custom therefore is ambivalent; it may be a sign of spiritual and moral independence, or it may be a sign of arbitrary subjectivism. In both cases it is the product of the emancipation of the individual from collectivity. On the other hand, it would be wrong to interpret the prevalence of social custom as spiritual inferiority and a defective sense of responsibility. Even a morally and spiritually mature man, who is perfectly willing to take full responsibility for his life, can acknowledge the necessity of social custom with regard to the common welfare. He would attribute to it the same function

[1] *Sitte*.

for society as to mechanical habit in individual life. It relieves life of unnecessary decisions and makes it free for decisions where they are really necessary. It would be stupid to deny the necessary function of individual habit. Without a great number of such habits, life is impossible. The same, the mature man might claim, is true of the function of social custom in society. He would add a second argument: to acknowledge the necessity of social custom is to acknowledge one's own limitations. Social custom may express the wisdom of the generations which is not consciously the wisdom of the individual. He would add a third argument: that not all people, if any, reach a state of complete moral maturity; and therefore people need the support of firm social custom. The necessity of social custom can be denied only by those who postulate that every individual be spiritually and morally awake at every moment, or who at least think that the absence of custom is more than compensated by the gain in individual responsibility.

At first sight it might appear that New Testament Christianity, which puts the highest obligation of personal responsibility on the individual, and which believes in a continual guidance by the Holy Spirit, would leave little room, if any, for social custom. But this is not so. Good customs are acknowledged and recommended; sometimes good custom is appealed to in order to end discussion. On the other hand, the apostles warn people against bad customs and demand a complete break with them. Therefore the man who was converted to the Christian faith had to break completely with pagan custom in order to become a member of the Church. By this break a vacuum of social custom was created. But this vacuum was filled by something else, by the order of life in the Christian community. This Christian order of life was a new kind of social custom. A body of rules, hardly conscious and never formulated, powerfully shaped the life of the individual Christian; its origin could hardly be traced and its necessity and rightfulness was never questioned. The importance of such Christian social custom in the early Church can harly be over-estimated. Certainly the great moral teachers of the early Church whose writings we know not only enjoined, but also verified and corrected, these social habits of the Christian community. The individual Christian, however, did do, or abstained from doing, many things differently from the rest of the world, for the sole reason that this was the social habit of the Church.

Because social habit is formed unconsciously, and by its very essence is beyond people's criticism, there is great danger of every good custom degenerating into bad custom or into mere convention. Furthermore, social habit sometimes has no other purpose than effectively to separate one social class from another. The Court nobility, the upper classes, develop special customs and even complete codes of behaviour from the mere instinct of exclusiveness. The function of these customs is to distinguish those who belong to the upper circles, and so to prevent others from intruding. In a similar way habits are formed in other sections of society which for other reasons wish to be distinguished and separated from the rest. Where this becomes conscious, such custom turns into a sort of private law.

Social habit is a most complex thing: primeval religious customs long forgotten, political and military measures, obsolete legal institutions, prescriptions of long abandoned techniques, survive as social habits. "Everybody does it"—without knowing why, even if it is apparently senseless. All the same, this conservatism of social habit is not merely social inertia, but an instinct for the preservative power and necessity of social habit in general. It is an instinct for the necessity of a certain irrational factor, of a rule of conduct, the meaning of which cannot be thoroughly grasped. That is why the typically enlightened man, who acknowledges as truth only what he can himself understand, naturally despises and opposes social custom. It seems to him unworthy to subject himself to a rule which he does not thoroughly understand. The age of the Enlightenment therefore was the time when social custom was cleared away, just as, about the same period, the old fortifications and towers of former centuries were cleared away in European cities, because they were merely obstacles to modern traffic. Indeed, how much old rubbish has been swept away since the

Enlightenment! How much easier to survey, and how much lighter, are our modern cities! How much more rational life has become!

If this parallel between architectural style and way of life holds good, the comparison will not be entirely in favour of the modern age. It can hardly be denied that the picture of a modern city is characterised by a complete lack of character and style. Architectural style is the expression of a common mind and feeling. In the age of a great style, even the simple workman builds well. The style builds for him. There is a more or less unconscious rule of building, directing the individual builder. The same is true of social habit: the age without style is also an age without custom. The individual is isolated, left to himself; there is no direction, no aim to be unconsciously followed. Everyone has to find his own style of life, and this is simply beyond him. The philosophy of the Enlightenment, being itself the heir of a great past, laid too heavy a burden upon the individual. The 17th and 18th centuries could indulge in an enthusiasm for freedom and emancipation without fearing chaos, because there were still the powerful integrating forces of the past, resisting chaotic dissolution. But in the 19th century the social structure begins to fall to pieces, and social chaos is waiting at the door which is opened in the 20th century; the reaction has already set in, in the shape of totalitarian compulsion.

In this present age, Western mankind vacillates between complete social dissolution and complete compulsion. Social custom as a uniting and controlling power has been reduced almost to nothing, apart from small groups of society. The individual is left to his own conscience and to his own good pleasure. No way of conduct is marked out for him. He has to decide for himself. Modern man has now begun to become disinclined for this super-abundance of personal responsibility; at the same time he is afraid of chaotic dissolution. From extreme individualism he swings over to a collectivist totalitarianism, finding it either in the Roman Catholic Church or in the Communist state. Protestantism, however, having identified itself wrongly with individualism, is no longer regarded as a spiritual power providing social cohesion and direction, because it was not capable of producing customs which would direct the individual without absolutely binding him. There is the same vacuum as in Protestant education, which we discussed in a previous lecture.

The less social custom, the more compulsory law. This truth needs no proof in the age of totalitarianism. Man, having lost the sense of direction in a time of complete freedom, turns to the opposite extreme, to that society in which everything is a matter of compulsion. It must be acknowledged, however, that the tremendous increase of the legal apparatus and the production of laws has other causes as well. Modern economic life has become so intense and complex that increased compulsory regulation became inevitable. The fast-growing world-traffic has made necessary, so to say, a universal traffic-police to lay down compulsory rules of social life.

This quantitative increase in state regulation, however, is not the only characteristic feature of recent times. Alongside it a qualitative change of greater importance is taking place, by which the totalitarian danger becomes imminent. In earlier times common law was a pre-state element, a fixed social relation. English common law is still independent of the state on the one hand, and hardly distinguishable from social custom on the other. For the Continental European of our time, English common law and the whole legal practice of England is very difficult to understand, because on the Continent common law has been displaced by codified law; the only remainder of common law there is what we call *Gewohnheitsrecht* (custom-law). But neither the term "common law" nor *Gewohnheitsrecht* tells the whole truth. In the German word *Recht* there is a reminiscence of the relation between law and justice or righteousness, which is lacking in the word "law". Common law in the English sense can exist only because and so long as there is a close relation between law and morality. On the other hand, the expression *Gewohnheitsrecht* is inadequate, because it is not a matter of mere custom, but of common moral conviction.

In older times the legal sense or consciousness, what we call *Rechtsbewusstsein,* was closely related to justice. Law had not yet the formal technical character which it has now. That is why the jurists of previous centuries could think of positive law as being merely a special form of natural law, so that there could be no real clash between the two. While the relation between law and justice or morality was obvious and close, the relation between law and state was much less obvious or acknowledged. Certainly the authority of the state was even then necessary to enforce law. But the king was rather the protector than the creator of law. The power of the state stands behind the common law to safeguard it, but law itself is, in principle, independent of the state. The idea that only by the state does a rule become law is entirely foreign to the people of older times, as it is still foreign to the English people.

Whatever may be the cause or causes of this change, the fact is undeniable that on the Continent law is understood by the jurists as meaning law of the state, and that the jurists consider the state to be the only source of law. It is probably the fact of the codification of common law in the early 19th century which has contributed more than anything else to this unfortunate development. In the same degree as law has been exclusively linked up with the state, it has lost its connection with social custom and morality. Everything which the state proclaims as a rule is *Recht,* whatever its moral quality may be. And nothing which the state does not proclaim as a rule is *Recht,* however just it may be. The close connection between *jus naturale* and *jus divinum* on the one hand and positive law on the other is in that way completely denied and disrupted.

This change has a double consequence. The first is a formalistic conception and development of law. Everything which the state declares to be a rule—all administrative machinery and procedure—is just as much law as those laws which order the conduct of the citizens and upon which rests the distinction between what is permitted and what is forbidden, what is lawful and what is unlawful. What in older times was *Recht* as distinguished from *Unrecht,* " lawful " as distinguished from " unlawful ", has now become a subordinate part of an immense body of administrative rules and prescriptions for business transactions. It is no more the content but the form which is decisive. All rules and regulations which the state places upon the statute book are considered as the one body of law; and thus the conception of law is formalised, and has almost completely lost its connection with justice and morality.

The second change is of even greater importance. Whatever the state declares as law is *Recht*, even if it is the very opposite of justice and morality. The state is no longer the protector, it is now the producer of law. The state is no longer under the law, but above it. As there is no law but that which the state gives, there is also no law above the state, by which the state can be called to account. There are no primary rights preceding the laws of the state, no human rights which the state has to acknowledge and which it cannot repeal. The state has become sovereign in a sense which in the Middle Ages was sometimes applied to the monarch: *princeps legibus solutus*. The state, being the only source of law, cannot but be itself *legibus solutus*. The state can declare as law whatever it likes, which means that the formalism of the new conception of law includes or leads to state absolutism. This new conception of law then has a marked tendency to totalitarianism. The totalitarian state of our time is the practical consequence of this development of the modern conception of law. What is to be said from the Christian point of view about this whole development of the conception of law?

Every reader of the Bible knows the close relation which exists between law and the divine will. The conception of *jus divinum*, divine law, is fundamental in Biblical thought. But if we try to formulate more clearly what this divine law is which so profoundly impresses us, particularly in the Old Testament, we are confronted with a series of most difficult and confusing questions. The *jus divinum* transcends all legal relations between men, being also the basis of purely moral and religious relations and conduct. In the Pauline concept of *dikaiosyne Theou* the element of divine mercy and forgiveness is essential, and the whole redemptive work of Christ is included. This new "righteousness" is the norm and essence of that relation between men which does not ask for justice but is based on spontaneous love, that love which Jesus in the Sermon on the Mount opposes to the attitude dictated by mere justice. For the same reason it is impossible, though it has so often been tried, to make the Decalogue the basis for legal justice, because the Decalogue is interpreted by our Lord to mean nothing else than that free spontaneous love which transcends all requirements of mere justice. And finally, the attempt to derive the divine law from the several codes of law in the Old Testament proves to be not very successful, because these laws were given to the people of Israel over more than a thousand years in its specific historical situation, which is so entirely different from ours.

As a matter of fact, the development of law and legal practice in the Western Christian world has, on the whole, not followed the line of biblicism, but has tried to make the *jus divinum* bear upon the legal reality by the concept of *jus naturale* or *lex naturae;* or, more exactly, by identifying this concept of ancient philosophy and jurisprudence with the Christian idea of *jus divinum*. During fifteen centuries this *jus naturale*, in its Biblical or Christian interpretation, was the foundation of juridical thinking in Europe, until in the age of the Enlightenment the Christian interpretation was replaced by a rationalistic one, and, in the time of romantic historicism and naturalistic positivism, the whole idea of a *jus naturale* was abandoned, and jurisprudence and political theory became devoid of any kind of normative principle, law becoming a matter of mere political power.

But this unfortunate development, resulting in the complete dissolution of the idea of natural law, had its origin—partly at least—in this concept itself, because from the beginning of its Christian history a double uncertainty or confusion was connected with it. First, it had never been made clear, either by theologians or by jurists, what was the distinction between the Christian and the pagan interpretation of *lex naturae*. Second, it had never become clear how *lex naturae* as the principle of juridical law was distinguished from Christian love as the principle of personal conduct. While it was certain that justice was not the same thing as love, nobody seemed to be capable of giving a clear definition or a theological justification of justice as distinct from love. It is here that our thinking has to start.

What is justice as distinct from love? And what is its theological foundation? Is there room for such justice within a Christian conception of God and of life? It is true that Jesus, laying down the rules of His kingdom, speaks of love only, calling it the "better righteousness". More than that, He interprets this love in sharpest distinction from seeking one's own rights, and from legalism. He does not, however, teach His disciples not to respect the rights of others. The love which He teaches includes this respect for our neighbours' rights, while far transcending it. Love that would not first give the other man what he has a right to claim is mere sentimentality, and provokes resentment on the part of one's fellow man. While love is higher than mere justice, it is inclusive of justice. Love, then, presupposes justice. Because this is so, there must be a divine norm for this justice, which therefore is the basis also of all human law. What is this norm?

Whoever says that a thing is just or unjust is thinking of something which belongs to man. Justice—in its distinction from love—is identical with "belonging", and this "belonging" is to be understood in a normative sense, independent of human laws. Justice presupposes a divine order of belonging, of whatever kind this belonging may be. This is the meaning of *lex naturae*, both in the pre-Christian and in the Christian sense. But within the Christian faith this order of belonging is not an order of "nature"—in the pantheistic sense of the word —but of God's creation. In creating anything, God gives it its own shape; He defines what belongs to its "rightness". In creating man, God says: "This and that belongs to man's life, this and that must not be taken away from man, but must be given to him. Man, whom I have created, has a claim to this and that, because I created him with this and that. To give it to him is just; not to give it to him is unjust." The basis of earthly justice, of legal order between men, is God's creation of man, in so far as it includes those things which belong to man and yet could, though unjustly, be taken away from him by his fellow men. In other words, the basis of the Christian conception of justice and law is the Christian conception of man.

And this is, as a matter of fact, what has been for centuries the foundation of the Christian understanding of law and justice; it is still that where it has not been destroyed or perverted by rationalism and—much worse—by naturalism and sceptical relativism. It is the Christian conception of man as a person, having from God's creation his divine origin and dignity, a person destined to have communion with other persons, a person-in-community. What distinguishes the legal structure of the "Christian" West from antiquity and from the rest of the world is this basic concept of person, this Biblical personalism. It hardly needs to be said that this Christian element has only been one of many which actually formed the laws and legal practices of the Western world. But even where it has not been dominant, it has still been effective as critical norm and standard.

The mere fact that we speak of "man", thus ignoring all differences of sex, age, race, class, etc., is a Christian heritage. In law this idea of "man as such" is of immediate practical importance, because it is on this idea that there rests what we call "equal right". When we read in our Swiss constitution— as probably in many others—"*jeder Schweizer ist vor dem Gesetze gleich*",[1] this is a direct consequence or application of the Christian idea of man. Whatever may be the practical legal consequences drawn from this principle, it is in itself a factor of the first magnitude.

It is closely related to a second idea which has exactly the same origin, the idea of "human rights" It is only in quite recent years that we have rediscovered the necessity and bearing of this concept. By it we mean that there are things belonging to man as such, rights which precede the state, which the state has to acknowledge, but which it cannot create, "birthrights of

[1] All Swiss are equal before the law.

manhood" founded on God's creation. It is this conception which distinguishes the lawful state from the totalitarian state. In the moment when these aboriginal human rights are denied or abolished by the state, the totalitarian state is there, at least in principle. That is why in the preceding parts of this lecture we have laid so much stress on the independence of law from the state. The human rights precede the state in order of dignity. The state is created for the protection of those human rights which man has not from the state but from the Creator.

It is only fair to admit that this principle of human rights and of the conception of "man as man" has its roots not only in the Christian but also in the Stoic conception of man: on that we dwelt in a lecture of the first series. The difference between the Stoic and Christian conceptions of "man as such", however, becomes clear in the fact that in Christian anthropology man is not conceived of merely as an independent individual, but as a "person-in-community". While Stoic and modern rationalism construed their philosophy of law and justice entirely from the standpoint of individual personality and therefore influenced the development of society in the direction of a thoroughgoing individualism, the Christian conception of man is characterised by a polarity of individual man and social community. Therefore the function of law is to safeguard not merely the rights of the individual, but at the same time those of the natural societies. Over against Stoic—or modern—individualism the Christian conception of justice stands for a communal personalism or, if you like, a personalistic socialism, in which the rights of the individual are limited by the rights of the community.

On the other hand, this limitation of the individual by the community is entirely different from, and strictly opposed to, collectivist subordination of the individual, particularly under the state. The human person, and man's personal rights, are derived from the same source as those of the communities. The individual is not a mere function or functionary of the community, of the state, but has his fundamental independence. In this respect the Christian conception of man, however different from individualistic liberalism, stands firm on the side of liberalism against all attempts of anonymous society or tyrannical state to degrade the person into a mere instrument of collective power.

There is, however, an even deeper root of Christian opposition to all kinds of tyranny: the principle of divine sovereignty. The first pronouncement about "belongings" or "rights" is this: that all things belong to God. The *jus divinum* is not in the first place the right which God gives, but the right which God has, and this right alone is absolute. The phrase which we read at the beginning of books printed in Great Britain, "All rights reserved" is—in its most serious and literal sense—what the principle of the Divine Sovereignty means. By it all human rights are—if I may use this ugly word—de-absolutised. While they are given by God, they are nevertheless not absolute. This principle of God's sovereignty is the surest, and in fact the only, safeguard against two great dangers: a false absolutism of the sovereignty of the people, leading to anarchy, and a false absolutism of the sovereignty of the state, leading to totalitarianism. It is no chance, then, that in an age which has largely forgotten the meaning of the sovereignty of God, mankind is wavering between these two evils, anarchic dissolution of law and order, and tyrannical totalitarian order.

The recognition of the sovereignty of God is, however, also a safeguard against a false absolutism of law itself. However firmly grounded these laws may be and must be, above all of them we read that inscription: "All rights reserved". There is no absolute human justice. There is no absolute human law. Therefore we should not attempt what the rationalist philosophers of natural law attempted: to deduce from the first principles of justice a whole system of laws of timeless validity. Human life, as seen by the Christian, is characterised by two traits which make this impossible, its transitoriness and its sinfulness. What was just yesterday may be unjust to-morrow, because of changed conditions. What might be just for people who are "angels" may be thoroughly unjust for people who are sinners. There is no possibility of construing a perfect order of law and justice from a few given principles.

The mistrust of all over-systematic doctrines of law and justice is well grounded, and we praise the English for their instinct in this matter. But this character of English legal tradition, which to us Continentals is at the same time so confusing and so attractive, is immune against a most deadly relativism only by reason of the strong infiltration of the *jus divinum* of the Christian tradition, and by the fact that the Christian conception of man is still alive.

There are two errors to be guarded against: deductive *a priori* constructions of systems, and relativistic opportunism. If we look back over the history of European law, we can observe quite distinctly that so long as Christian tradition was truly alive and dominant, there were no such systems of law as began to be developed by the rationalists of the 18th century. To-day, however, the second danger is much greater: that all divine foundation, norm, and sanction of law should disappear in the general trend of relativism and naturalism. The positivistic school of law, which has prevailed in Europe for almost a century, is largely responsible for the legal chaos and the totalitarian monstrosity.

There is one last reason why we need a foundation of law in the *jus divinum*. Only where a glimmer of divine light shines through the legal order of a nation can spontaneous obedience be expected. Where the opinion becomes prevalent that law is nothing but human invention, a sum of decisions taken by political powers, or where the justice of the law disappears under an immensity of technical regulations, the people will not obey law spontaneously, but only because and in so far as they are afraid of enforcement. And where this condition prevails, more and more laws have to be made and more and more force must be used. We can escape the totalitarian state machinery only by the vigour of spontaneous obedience, and therefore only by a sense of the sacredness of the legal order. Happy that people which can count upon this attitude of free obedience; and woe to that people which has lost it.

IX
POWER

AS the word "power" has many meanings, we want to make plain from the start that by power we here understand the capacity of man to determine the life, i.e. the doing and the not-doing, of others, by compulsion. In a very strict sense, compulsion is impossible; even the mightiest and most cruel tyrant can compel no one to do his will, if the other man does not want to obey, but rather suffers the consequences of disobedience. In our time, however, scientific cruelty has brought us near the point where even this last resort of human freedom is eliminated. But in that case man as a human being is also eliminated and turned into an automaton.

Apart from these two extremes, compulsion can be exerted by many means, and the sum of these available means we call power. A father can compel his children because they are dependent on him, or because he is physically stronger, or because his parental authority is granted by law and state. A teacher has power over his pupils, the "boss" has power over his employees, an officer over his men, a judge over the culprit. In a well-ordered state, the judge can be sure that the state will use all its means of compulsion in order to guarantee the carrying out of his sentence. The state has power over every single citizen and over every group of citizens. It can compel them to do what they do not like doing. The great powers amongst the nations are those that can, if they wish, subjugate the small ones to their will, either directly or indirectly. To *have* power does not necessarily mean to *use* it, though its mere existence has an effect similar to its actual use wherever it is uncertain how this power will be used.

Power over others is desired by most men for two reasons. First, power over another man is, so to say, a reduplication of one's own existence. Instead of one, I have two human organisms at my disposal. I can make the other work and live for me without worrying about his life beyond his utility for me. The second reason is of a more inward nature. Power means also enhancement of value, prestige, whether in my own estimation or in that of others. We therefore understand why men desire power, and why few who have it abstain from using it, whether in the first, more objective, or in the second, more subjective, sense.

Power is the more desirable as the goods of this world are already portioned out, because by power this distribution can be changed in favour of the one who has power. That is why a large part of human life is a struggle for power or the use of power in the struggle for goods. This power and its use can take various shapes. Everything by which the capacity to compel is increased can become a means of power: bodily strength and ability, shrewdness in putting one's own superiority into action in the right place, possession of things that others must have or desire to have; and these things can be of the most different kinds: economic goods, the keys of Heaven or doors to the high places in society or state. It is impossible to separate physical power from spiritual, even with regard to compulsion. The power of the state, for instance, by which it can compel the citizens, is not merely, nor even predominantly, the police and military force which stand behind its commands; it is composed of innumerable factors, the sum of which may be called the spiritual authority of the state.

Because power is the capacity to compel, it stands in direct opposition to freedom. The power of one over the other is the dependence of the second on the first. Power and freedom are related as the convex to the concave. The surplus of freedom of the one, which is power, is the deficit of freedom of the other. Power creates dependence. But not all dependence is created by power, because there exists also dependence out of free will. Furthermore, a dependence created by power may become spontaneous. The good citizen of a good state wants the state to be powerful. He accepts its compulsive power with his free will. The freely chosen leader of a group has power which the group accepts and which therefore is not felt as compulsion. This freely willed power must not be confused with a merely psychic dependence or bondage, which is a strange mixture of acceptance and refusal of power.

Because power, taken by itself, is opposed to freedom, there is a tendency in every society to order and to canalise power in order to limit its danger for the less powerful. The most important means to order power is law, which in itself is nothing but "ordered power" or "order of power". It is a necessity of civilised life that the ultimate use of power, the power over the lives of others, be centralised. This centralisation of ultimate power is the state. It originates from the necessity to localise ultimate power in a few hands and to canalise it by certain rules. What we call state is the centralised monopoly of exerting ultimate power. Power, not merely social organisation, is the characteristic essence of the state. The *social* organisation of society is in itself something very "harmless". The state, however, begins at the moment when this harmlessness disappears, i.e. when behind this social organisation an institution stands with ultimate power, power over men's lives. This instrument, the state, is necessary as a safeguard of peace because it is only this monopoly of ultimate power that checks the tendency of men to use their powers to the utmost limit for their own benefit, up to the point of killing. The will-to-power, and recklessness in using it are so strong in man that again and again he does not hesitate to kill. Until this possibility is taken away by the monopoly of ultimate power by the state, peaceful civilised life cannot develop. In this sense the state is the presupposition of cultural life.

This centralisation of ultimate power in the state, however, is only one step in taming the dangerous power-element. The second step is the ordering of centralised power by law. Ultimate power and the power of the state in general must be exerted only within definite limits, and for definite purposes, and in a definite manner. The power of the state should only be used in the service of the life of the people and in defence of their rights. The state must be the guarantee of peace, order and justice. We have seen in the preceding lecture that the state is not the source of law, but rather its guarantee. The state is the servant of man and not their master. Its *raison d'être* is to protect the lives and the rights of men. That is why the monopoly of ultimate power is given to it. State-law is primarily law for the state and not law of the state. State-law is the limitation and canalisation of the power of the state. We call it public law, in distinction from private law, which the power of the state has to protect. It is by public law that society orders and disciplines the dangerous, though necessary, power of the state which is monopolised ultimate power. The rights of individuals and their lawful relations are not created by the state, but they are publicly acknowledged and protected by the coercive power of the state.

A third step, however, is necessary in order to guarantee this purpose of the state. This third step is the plurality of the bearers of power in the state what we call the division of power. This was the meaning in creating parliament, and this also was the meaning of a much older institution: courts independent of government. The absolute monarch united all state functions in his person. He was ruler, law-giver and judge. Yet the principle of "division of powers" is much older than Montesquieu; Montesquieu was merely the first who clearly recognised its importance. Already in the people of Israel there existed a certain division of powers; law was not given by the king, but by God through prophets and priests, and the king had to obey and to protect this law. The Roman Republic represents a well-thought-out division of powers, which was the result of century-long struggles. Montesquieu's principle, *le pouvoir arrête le pouvoir*, is the most essential element of a constitutional state, as distinct from absolutism and tyranny.

Whilst it would not be true to the facts to claim that the conception of power set forth in the preceding pages is exclusively Christian, it certainly *is* deeply rooted in the Christian faith. The sovereignty of God excludes an absolute of human power. It excludes both the absolute sovereignty of the state and the absolute sovereignty of the people. All human sovereignty is limited by divine sovereignty and by divine law. Furthermore, the Christian conception of sin reveals the dangers inherent in power. The Christian knows better than anyone else the temptation to misuse which is inherent in great power. Power is misused wherever it is used against the law of God and contrary to its God-given purpose.

When St. Paul deduces the power of the state from divine order and enjoins Christians to obey it, he is not thinking of the absolute sovereignty of state or monarch. The divine origin of the power of the state (*exousia*) is at the same time divine limitation. According to St. Paul this limitation is given with the purpose of the state, which is peace and justice. In stressing the power of the sword as a means of divine vengeance St. Paul gives that interpretation of the state as monopolised ultimate power which we have just been sketching. By this reference to the power of the sword the state is not reduced to the police function as has often been said. This reference to the sword is rather an expression of Biblical realism with regard to the *basic* elements of the state. It shows that the monopoly of ultimate power is the very essence of the state, as a basis for peaceful civilised life. This conception of state and power is correlative with the Biblical conception of sin. Wherever the power of sin and the temptation to sin, inherent in power, is seen, it becomes impossible to regard the state as a mere social organisation, as is done on the basis of an optimistic view of the nature of man.

The need for the concentration and canalisation of power in the state is so much the greater as there are great accumulations of power within society. Society does not consist of individuals merely, but of groups, some of which wield tremendous power. In our capitalist age there are concentrations of financial and industrial power, compared with which the individual is powerless. The credit system, combined with industrialisation, has produced an accumulation of economic power unknown in previous times: "big business", mammoth corporations controlling billions of dollars and hundreds of thousands of men, capable of limiting their freedom in a large measure, dominating the economic life and welfare of whole nations, and influencing the state machinery in a dangerously high degree. By their more or less monopolistic character, they exert an almost state-like coercive power.

This, however, is only one side of the picture. On the other side we see accumulations of power created by organisation of those who individually are powerless, i.e. the ever-growing power of trade unions and trade-union associations which in some countries has become equal to that of their capitalistic counterparts. Experience has proved that the great numbers of men associated in an organisation are at least equal in power to great wealth and, in the long run, even superior. By the development of these two concentrations of power, a new danger originates. These colossi, both business corporations and trade-union federations, have become, so to say, states within the state, being capable of challenging the state and thereby endangering its primary purpose. The purpose of the state is to serve the interests of all. Those economic mammoth organisations, however, are so powerful that they are able to force the state to do their will against public welfare. This situation explains in part why so many are intent upon strengthening the economic power of the state and are calling for a general state-control and even nationalisation of economy.

The last decades, however, have confronted us with a phenomenon more dangerous than any other to freedom and general welfare: the totalitarian state. The more comprehensive the state, the more dangerous its power. The democratic and liberal movement sprang from the desire to combat the danger that lay in state absolutism at a time when state absolutism was represented by the absolute monarch. Parliament and constitutional government were an effective attempt to bridle it. Since then monarchy has either disappeared or been eliminated as the bearer of power. Since the French Revolution the democratic principle of the "sovereignty of the people" has conquered the Western world. The rise of the totalitarian state—beginning in 1917—created a new situation. It is only now that we are beginning to see that the sovereignty of the people, manifesting itself in the election of the government by the people, is not in itself a safe guarantee against a new kind of state absolutism. It is possible to conceive a totalitarian state on a democratic basis. To think of democracy and totalitarianism as opposites is just as wrong as to identify totalitarianism with dictatorship. State-totalitarianism is not a form of government. The form of a state decides how and by whom political power is to be wielded. Totalitarianism, however, means the extension of political power over the totality of life whatever may be the form of government. The nationalisation of economy is the decisive step to this totality of political control over the totality of life. If neither individuals nor groups have independent economic means, they do not have real political freedom. If everyone is a functionary of the state, and if nobody can make his living independently of the state machinery, if there are no other than state schools, if the press, the cinema, the radio, are state controlled, free society is lost, opposition and public expression of independent opinion become impossible. Every deviation from the programme of the state becomes rebellion and sabotage. Even if this state has a democratic form, i.e. government elected by the majority vote of the people, it amounts to a complete suppression of liberty, and it will not be long before even the so-called free elections become illusory, the state machinery controlling all means of propaganda.

Compared with this modern totalitarian state, the absolute monarchy of old times looks rather innocent, because even under the most absolute monarch private property of individuals and groups, and the absence of state-controlled education and public opinion, left a considerable area open for free decision. In the totalitarian state, however, this area of free decision hardly exists, and therefore a free development of cultural life is almost totally excluded. For cultural self-expression is dependent on material means, and all these material means are in the hands of the state. To take one example: if the state decides who is to get the paper available for printing, can we believe that an opposition press could exist? The totalitarian state even controls the time of every individual citizen. No one can say: I prefer to earn less in order to have time for this or that cultural, moral or religious activity. State economy can exist only if it has complete control of the working time of everybody. Furthermore, it is the state that dictates for what things money may be or may not be spent. It not only controls schools and universities, but also the schools and exhibitions of art, and the theatre, all artists and actors being state employees. While in theory it is not forbidden to do, apart from matters of national importance, whatever one likes, this theoretical freedom is illusory, because it is the state alone which has the financial means necessary for any cultural activity. All this means that totalitarianism, even in a democratic form, is the grave of freedom.

Furthermore, even a democratic totalitarian state must necessarily degenerate because its power is unlimited. It produces an all-powerful bureaucracy of functionaries and a semi-militaristic hierarchy. This hierarchy necessarily has a monarchical top. The principle of the division of power becomes illusory. Its place is taken by the rivalry of the different sections of the state machinery, but all of them are dependent on the self-same pinnacle of the bureaucratic hierarchy. The democratic drama will still be played while actually there is a tyrannical dictatorship. All this is not merely a description of one of the totalitarian systems of the present time: these things are all the necessary and inevitable results of the complete nationalisation of economy. We have seen in recent years how—whether we like it or not—a war-time economy produces almost necessarily the worst features of totalitarianism: secret police, administrative jurisdiction, control of public opinion, etc., and that even within states with deeply rooted democratic tradition and with democratic institutions intact, complete state control of economy leads to the militarisation of the life of a nation.

For all these reasons the totalitarian state, being the absolute maximum of accumulated power, is the worst and most dangerous social evil which we can conceive. It is the Satanic incarnation of our time. Whatever analogies totalitarianism may have had in previous centuries, real totalitarianism has become possible only in our age, in which the techniques of production and transport, the aeroplane, the radio and the machine-gun, have made state power omnipresent, all-powerful and all-pervasive.

We have now to turn to a last and no less gloomy aspect of the power problem: the power-relation between the states. Mankind has somehow succeeded in eliminating the most destructive effects of power within a given territory by concentrating ultimate power in the state. Man has succeeded furthermore in bridling the state-power itself by law and constitutional division of power. In recent times, however, the formation of a few powerful states has created a new problem: the struggle for power between the major states, endangering the life and freedom of humanity. Thus far all attempts to bring the power-relations of the states under the control of justice and humanitarian interests have been almost without effect.

It may be said that in times when the divine law and the moral order exerted considerable influence on the nations and their rulers, this purely spiritual limitation of power exerted a certain smoothing and muffling influence. The states, however ruthless in their international behaviour, did not quite do everything lying within their power. By treaties they created a kind of international law, which proved effective to a certain extent, although its effects were limited by the fact that the treaties could not be enforced. For this reason modern man created institutions of international justice and peace, like the Court of the Hague, and the League of Nations, which were intended to replace the use of power by law. These institutions, however, proved incapable of solving the most important and dangerous conflicts arising from the dynamic character of history because they were limited by the principle of the sovereignty of the individual states. The League of Nations was certainly an attempt to limit individual state sovereignty by a supra-national federal structure. But this attempt proved futile because the great powers did not really intend to abandon their sovereignty to the will of the federation, and because some of the most powerful states were not members of the League. Horrified by the disastrous results of the second world war, the nations made a second attempt in the same direction by forming the United Nations Organisation. Although only a few years have elapsed since its formation, it must be admitted that this second attempt has also failed for the present. A condition of international anarchy therefore still prevails, leaving the feeble nation at the mercy of the powerful, and threatening humanity with a new conflagration which, should it become a reality, would most probably mean the end of human civilisation.

There remains the question of a world state. Why should it not be possible to overcome world-wide international anarchy in a way similar to that in which it has been overcome within a given territory by the little Swiss or by the big American federation, which combine regional autonomy with the overarching supremacy of the federation? Apart from the fact that such a proposal is purely academic for the present and for the near future, the question remains whether such a universal world state, having the monopoly of ultimate power, would not be the greatest danger to freedom and higher culture. Only a federal structure, combined with a strict division of powers, would prevent it from degenerating into tyranny. A centralised nonfederative, or, if I may use the phrase, a monolithic, world state would necessarily become a monster power of totalitarian character, whereas a federal structure always involves a certain risk for the peace of the world.

A truly Christian solution of the power problem, in either its economic, political or international aspect, does not seem to be a realistic prospect. The idea of a reign of peace and justice, in which the lust for power would not only be tamed, but be overcome from within, cannot materialise in a world of sinful men. There are not a few who do believe in such an earthly paradise. Probably they do not realise that such a hope implies one of two things. Either they have to assume that within this temporal world sin, that is lust for power, can be overcome, or they do not see that real peace is irreconcilable with sin. Both these views contradict the Christian conception of man and history.

Because as Christians we see the close connection between power and sin, we accept St. Paul's idea that only by monopolised ultimate power, i.e. by the state, can sinful anarchy be overcome. Whether it will be possible at some time to overcome the anarchy between the powerful states themselves by subordinating them to a super-power without endangering justice and freedom, we cannot know, though we may hope for it.

A short word may be added about the relation between power and culture. We cannot follow Jakob Burckhardt, who in his *Weltgeschichtliche Betrachtungen* opposes power to culture and makes culture, so to speak, the innocent martyr of power. How often has it happened that the most generous patrons of science and art have been also most ruthless in their power politics, misusing their power. It is not culture, it is only respect for justice, love, and reverence for the divine law, that are capable of overcoming the lust for and the misuse of power. It is only that mind which would rather suffer an injustice than perform it, and which is willing to "overcome evil with good", that is capable of resisting the temptation even of very great power. The greater the power, the greater the temptation of being godlike. Against this temptation no education or culture can prevail. The demon of power is overcome only by Jesus Christ. Therefore the most important thing that can be done at any time against the evil effects of the power motive is the spreading and deepening of true Christ-discipleship. The most dreadful thing, however, is the will-to-power in a Christian disguise, of which Western history is full. It is here, if anywhere, that we can see the cunning of the devilish power taking the shape of an angel of light, and thereby hiding the One who alone is capable of driving out the spirit of power.

We started our discussion with a definition of power, limiting its meaning to "the capacity to compel". We said that this use of the word was not the only possible one. We speak now of power in a sense which is far removed from this one. The multiplicity of meanings is not a matter of mere chance. Power in the most general sense is that which is capable of moving, particularly of moving us human creatures. There is a kind of power which moves us not by compulsion but by conviction. An idea may prove powerful—*idée force*. Such power, while it moves us, does not impinge upon our free action. On the contrary, such power makes us free. As Christians we speak of the power of God moving us by His spirit of truth and holy love. The apostles preached the gospel of Christ as the saving power of the world, as that power which beyond all others makes man free, giving him and revealing to him the truth of his own being, creating him as a free personality.

Christianity has proved a power in history. The gospel moved men to do what had never been done before and to refrain from doing what had always been done before; it moved them to suffer and to love, to rise above the level of the all-too-human and yet to remain human, nay, to become truly human by love and obedience to the divine will. Wherever the Christian faith in its New Testament purity has been present in individuals, in groups, in peoples, new things have happened, by the power of God. The greatest proof of this power of God is that it overcomes the lust for power, and thereby becomes a genuinely new factor in political life. Whether this happens very often or not is not the immediate question. We know, both from the teaching of the New Testament and from Christian experience, that wherever Christian faith is alive this does happen, sometimes in a lesser, sometimes in a higher, and sometimes in the highest and most conspicuous degree. And this is therefore the one bright feature in the picture: that Christian faith, love of God, and love of one's fellow man, does act as a political factor inasmuch as it works against the misuse of political power and works for that use of political power which is for the common good. It is natural, it is even inevitable, for Christians to hope that the influence of this Christian motive may become so great that solutions of political power problems which otherwise are insoluble become possible.

In the field of political action—which is a field of dynamics—numbers count, and therefore combination of human wills for concerted action counts. The Christian community or Church has in itself a principle of community inseparable from Christian faith. It has therefore a chance in the political field—in the field of " power ", in the first sense of the word—to influence the course of history, provided that it is pure, strong and united. If it is not pure, it will become powerful in the bad sense of the word, and will lust for that power; if it is not strong, it cannot compete in the field where power is decisive; if it is not united, it has little chance to influence the political course of history. There is no reason to deny the possibility that the Christian faith, in its original purity and unity and strength, might again become such a reality that it could change the gloomy picture of the political scene. There is every reason for Christians to pray and to work that this may happen, because unless it does happen it is most probable that the prospects of our civilisation will become gloomier still.

X

THE CHRISTIAN IDEA OF CIVILISATION AND CULTURE

WE have spoken so far, in the first series of these lectures, about the foundation of civilisation, and in the earlier lectures of this series about some spheres of civilised or cultural life. We now go back to the question with which we started: what is a Christian civilisation? We have seen how problematic this concept is. We have stated that there never was in a strict sense a Christian civilisation, and that what is usually called by that name is a compromise between Christian and non-Christian forces. We have now come to the point where it may be possible to sketch something like the Christian idea of civilisation or culture. By the two terms, civilisation and culture, we understand something typically and exclusively human; man alone is capable of producing it. Whatever astonishing analogies may be found in the life of animals—the beaver-dam, the state of the ants, the so-called language and games of the animals—they are mere analogies and not beginnings of cultured and civilised life because they are all tied to biological necessities, as nourishment, procreation and shelter. Man alone can transcend these necessities by his creative imagination, and by the idea of something which is not yet but ought to be; by the ideas of the good, of justice, beauty, perfection, holiness and infinitude. It is true that even human civilisation and culture are related to biological necessity and have their basis within natural organic life which is common to us and the animals. But even where man is tied to biological necessity he acts in a way which transcends mere utility and gives his doings a human stamp. He does not " feed " like the animals, he eats; he ornaments his vessels, his instruments, his house, he establishes and observes fine customs, he explores truth irrespective of utility, he creates beautiful things for the sheer joy of beauty. He orders his relations according to ideas of justice and liberty. He masters power by law, he sacrifices time, energy and life for ideas and ideals. All this is civilisation and culture. Therefore we can define them as that formation of human life which has its origin not in mere biological necessity but in spiritual impulses. Wherever spirit, transcending the physical urge, enters the scene of life as a formative force, there civilisation and culture comes into existence.

These spiritual impulses and formative forces are of the most varied kinds. The impulse to create the beautiful, to realise justice, to know the truth, to preserve the past, to enter into spiritual communication, to invent the new, to extend the range of human intercommunion, to share the sufferings and joys of others; the impulse to submit the totality of life to ultimate directives and give it a meaning, unity and intelligibility, and finally to place everything under the divine will and receive it from the hands of God—all these are impulses out of which culture and civilisation arise.

All the same, we should not idealise culture and civilisation, as is done so often. These spiritual motives, although transcending biological necessity, are mixed with egoism, lust for power, and ambition. They are in competition with each other, one motive trying to displace the others and to monopolise life. Artistic or scientific impulses can be mixed with irresponsibility, inhuman hardness and brutality. The scientist can be blind to art, the artist to science, and both can be indifferent to moral or religious truth. Religion can become fanatical and cruel, it can hamper or even cripple art, science, technics, community, by its prejudices. Although all these spiritual elements transcend the biological urge, none of them as such is a guarantee of true, full humanity. Everyone of them can become a parasite in relation to the others, or an idol, or a caricature. The intensity and height of cultural achievement therefore is no sure mark of a truly human life. Intensity can be in conflict with harmony or totality. And this conflict can assume the most evil and ugliest forms of the struggle for life. Spiritual energy, combined with lust for power and egoism, gives the animal instincts a demoniac power unknown in the animal realm. The means which technics and organisation, planning and association, give to the human will, can produce a kind of civilisation which, although it is still characteristic of man, can lead into catastrophes that may amount to a suicide of humanity.

All these dark aspects belong to the character of human civilisation, which is the civilisation of sinful men. Civilisation and culture, then, are not in themselves the opposite of evil and depravity. They can become the very instruments of evil and negative forces, as they have always been to a certain extent. Culture and civilisation, although they belong exclusively to man, are not in themselves *the* truly human. True, without culture and civilisation man cannot be human, but in themselves they do not guarantee the truly human character of life. That is what we have called, in a previous connection, the formal character of civilisation. Wherever spirit expresses itself, there is civilised life; but what kind of a spirit creates that civilisation or culture is another question. Culture is an expression of the spirit, a formation by spiritual impulse, but this spiritual impulse can originate from the most different sources, and therefore is no guarantee of inner unity.

The question then arises whether there exists a spiritual impulse capable of relating all the other impulses in the right proportions and unifying them in such a way as to produce a truly human life. Does there exist an understanding of man which gives to all the elements of human life—the biological, economic, technical, scientific, artistic, individual, social and communal—their full chance, and which at the same time subdues all of them to that which guarantees true humanity? Furthermore, is this understanding of man, if it exists, of such a kind that it is capable of functioning as an organising dynamic, so that it is not a mere idea but a directing power? As a result of our investigations we can give a positive answer to these questions. This conception of man is implicit in the Christian faith in its New Testament purity and dynamic.

The Christian faith alone views man as a spiritual-bodily unit whose powers and impulses, originating from his physical nature and from his spiritual disposition, are all co-ordinated in such a way that they are subordinated to a human destiny which transcends both the natural and the spiritual life, and is directive of both. "All are yours, and ye are Christ's, and Christ is God's." "Of every tree of the garden thou mayest freely eat"—only from the tree in the middle of the garden, the tree of the divine mystery, by reservation of the holy God, man shall not eat. All that is creature is in a specific way subordinated to man, but he himself with all his life and powers is subordinated to God who is holy love and who destines men for communion with Himself and with each other. Man is created to subdue and have dominion over all creation, but "whether you eat or drink or whatsoever you do, do all to the glory of God". This is the programme of life given to men by the Creator: free development of all their powers, free use of all the means under the dominion of the One who gives all and ordains all to Himself.

Now, before we go on to enlarge this Biblical idea of culture, some questions have to be taken up which obtrude themselves from the standpoint of history. As we have seen, in our first lecture, the New Testament shows very little interest in the specific tasks of civilisation and culture. How then can faith, which seems so indifferent to culture, be its basis? Our answer is twofold. First, it is true that the main concern of the New Testament message is not culture or civilisation, not the temporal but the eternal, not the earthly but the heavenly life. The Gospel is not focussed on culture, but on the world-to-come. "This world passes away", and with it civilisation. Christian faith, indeed, is alive only where the life with God in Christ and the eternal kingdom of God is the centre of interest. "Seek ye first His kingdom and His righteousness." The kingdom of God is not human civilisation. It stands above both the physical and the cultural life. That is the first thing which has to be said. The second point, however, which must be repeated, is that this perspective of the kingdom of God does not alienate men from their temporal life. Faith in the kingdom and in eternal life does not make men indifferent to the tasks which earthly existence lays upon them. On the contrary, the Christian is summoned to tackle them with special energy, and his faith gives him the power to solve these problems better than he could without faith. "Seek ye first the kingdom of God ... and these things shall be added unto you." It is precisely the man whose first concern is not culture but the kingdom of God that has the necessary distance from cultural aims and the necessary perspective to serve them in freedom, and to grasp that order which prevents the various sections of civilisation from monopolising the totality of life. Only from beyond civilisation can its order and harmony come.

It is a humanistic superstition to believe that the man to whom culture is everything is the true bearer of culture. The opposite is true. Culture necessarily degenerates where it is made God. Culture-idolatry is the sure road to cultural decay. If culture is to become and to remain truly human, it must have a culture-transcending centre. Man is more than his culture. Culture is means and tool, but not the essence of human life. It is not culture that gives man his humanity, but it is the human man that creates a human culture. That is why it is a grave error to think that the Christian faith is the enemy of culture, or at least indifferent to it, because it so emphatically accentuates the culture-transcending centre of life.

But what is the verdict of history? I think that, correctly interpreted, it confirms what has just been said. It is true that there have been Christian movements showing a kind of cultural asceticism, that there have been times when faith and theological interest absorbed men to such a degree that they neglected their cultural obligations. It is true that the Christian Church has sometimes obstructed the development of science or other cultural functions. While we are not justified in taking these negative facts too lightly, we are obliged on the other hand to beware of rash inferences. We have always to make sure first whether it is really Christian faith that acts, and secondly whether it is really cultural values that are at stake. In Occidental history so many things have usurped the name of

"Christian" which were only half Christian or pseudo-Christian. On the other hand, so many things have been postulated in the name of cultural necessity that were pseudo-cultural. Because it is of the nature of sin that one branch of life wants to develop at the cost of another equally important, and because it is a temptation for the cultured man to idolise culture and thereby deprive it of its truly human character, it must always be the foremost interest of the Christian to proclaim faith and love as the source and norm of all true humanity. By doing this, he does, in the long run, the best service to culture.

Finally, there is always a certain tendency in cultural humanism to understand spirit and culture in such a way that so-called "higher" culture becomes detached from every-day life, from marriage and family, from civic order and from social obligations. Such a humanism is inclined to forget that the soundness of family life is the basis of all true civilisation, that justice and freedom in public life are necessary presuppositions of all higher culture. There is a certain aristocracy of spirit which has little interest in popular education, or in the task of giving a real meaning to the work of the ordinary man, and which focusses all its interest on science, art and so-called higher culture. Such an attitude proves detrimental to real culture. It is at this point that the importance of the Christian view of life becomes particularly obvious. All this makes the question of the relations between historical Christianity and civilisation so complicated that it is hardly possible to reach a final judgment. On one point, however, we can speak without reserve: the history of civilisation during the last hundred years has made clear beyond any doubt that the progressive decline of Christian influence has caused a progressive decay of civilisation. But even that may remain doubtful to one who personally has no understanding of what Christian faith means.

These preliminaries being settled, we can now proceed to develop a little further the Christian idea of culture and civilisation. We start from the statement that human culture presupposes human man. It is not culture that makes man human, but it is human man who makes culture human. This order of things is given with the Christian faith. Man comes first, not civilised life. Man becomes human, not by culture and civilisation, but by understanding his human destiny. In the Christian revelation the destiny of man is love. The measure of culture is personality; more exactly, person-in-communion. Creative individuality is no equivalent of personal life in community. God is love—that is the centre of the Christian message, and this doctrine is exclusively Christian. Love is the first and the last, the ultimate reality, being the very essence of God. Love is not one amongst others, not one virtue alongside other virtues; love is no virtue at all: it is true humanity, as it is the essence of God. This love, *agapé* in the New Testament sense, is no natural disposition. It is acquired by faith. Man is created for this love: that is why he has a longing for it. But in spite of this natural longing, man does not have it by birth, he has to receive it as a supernatural gift. By this, his eternal destiny, man is culture-transcending. The meaning of his life is not in culture; on the contrary, it is his task to express and to realise this culture-transcending destiny in his cultural life. Culture then is means, expression, tool of true humanity, but not its origin and aim.

The first consequence of this conception of life is that the most important thing in life is the relation between man and man. Therefore it is not impersonal spiritual activity, it is not spiritual creation as such, but it is the formation of truly personal social relationships, which is the basis of true culture. There is more real culture in a truly human family life without art and science than in the highest achievements of art and science on the basis of neglected family life and degenerate sex-relations.

The second consequence of Christian anthropology is the acknowledgment of man's bodily-spiritual unity. In contrast with idealistic humanism, Christian faith does not despise the body and the bodily needs. The Christian doctrine of incarnation obliges the Christian to take the body and its needs seriously, and gives him the double task of incorporating the spirit and spiritualising the bodily life. Spirituality detached from the concerns of the body contradicts the Biblical doctrine of creation and produces an abstract kind of culture. The Christian understanding of corporal-spiritual unity has two consequences. First, it places the body under the direction of the spirit. Second, it takes seriously the problems of manual work, economy and material property. From this point of view a decent and meaningful order of every-day life and healthy economic conditions are important criteria of true civilisation. A well-ordered estate, with dignified houses of simple beauty and a carefully-managed farm, is a surer indication of true culture than a marvellous university, a famous academy of art, in the midst of a peasant or industrial proletariat. The Christian ethos has—paradoxical as this may appear—a strongly *bourgeois* trait, if we understand this word in its original sense of well-ordered citizenship. In the New Testament, eschatology—which certainly is the very opposite of anything *bourgeois*—is combined with a sober and earnest ethic of work and an intention to equalise social conditions. One might say with Kierkegaard, that this *bourgeois* element is the necessary outward incognito of the essentially anti-bourgeois heart and mind of the Christian.

The primacy of personal relations, as distinguished from purely abstract spiritual creativity, has another important consequence. In the Christian conception of sin it is not sensuality but egoism and pride which hold the first place. That is why those dangers which come from lust of power are taken most seriously, and why a high premium is placed upon good government and public justice. Social relations cannot be in accordance with human dignity if this lust for power is not kept within firm barriers in economic as well as in political life. To lead a truly human life, man must have an intangible sphere of freedom guaranteed by law. For this reason the Christian must regard civic order, security, and a certain homogeneity in the sphere of economics, as an important criterion of cultural soundness. Wherever public institutions give evidence of the will to form human life as a community of free personalities, there is culture.

From the same source derives the high valuation of tradition and social custom. These conservative forces, which limit the freedom of the individual, however, are not without strong counter-weights, originating from the Christian hope of a new world. It may be said, perhaps, that in the Christian view of a good life the conservative elements are stressed so much because otherwise the eschatological perspective of the Christian faith might lead to an illusionist revolutionary attitude. On the other hand, tradition and social custom are an expression of the sense of responsibility and mutual obligation. They represent the element of solidarity and loyalty, helping the individual—if they are not stressed too much—to acquire mature independence.

One of the most obvious contributions of Christianity to civilised life is its pre-eminent interest in education and instruction. Again, the Christian view of education is characterised by its personalism. It is not knowledge and ability which stand in the first rank, but education of responsible personality and social training. Wherever Christian tradition has been alive, it has influenced the educational life of the nations in this direction. In contrast with it, the dechristianisation of Continental Europe, as the result first of an abstract spiritualism of a humanistic type and later on of materialistic utilitarianism, have resulted in an almost complete neglect of the personal and social element in education, and in the preponderance of abstract educational aims, such as knowledge and professional ability. Pestalozzi's idea of education, deeply rooted in the Christian understanding of life, and therefore putting responsible personality and love in the first place, has been entirely misunderstood or neglected, in spite of its fame.

It is only in the last place in a Christian programme of civilisation that we find what in the humanistic programme comes first: the so-called higher culture, embracing the purely spiritual elements, such as science and art. The expression, "higher culture", is justified in so far as in this realm the activity of the spirit is most remote from animalic urge and biological necessity. It is also, and for the same reason, the field of a spiritual *élite*. It is the realm of spiritual creativity. While in principle everyone can be good, only a few can be creative; the creative genius is the exception, and it is he who produces the works of which we mostly think when speaking of culture. It is, however, characteristic of the Christian conception of culture and civilisation to give these peak manifestations less importance than does idealistic humanism, for it is not science, art and spiritual activity which give life its truly human content, but love.

This specific order of values, however, does not prevent the Christian from giving art and science, as well as so-called higher education, a characteristic aim and meaning. Science as the search for truth, and art as the creation of the beautiful, are given the highest possible meaning: divine service. Wherever truth is known, something of the mystery of creation is revealed. The true scientist is a servant of God. To know and to acknowledge God is not a hindrance but, on the contrary, a help, in the search for truth. It keeps us from false absolutism and relativism, from idolatry of reason, and from sceptical despair. The scientist working, like Kepler, under highest command and for the honour of God is free from mean ambition and jealousy. The same is true of the artist. There is nothing which ennobles and purifies his creative powers so much as the conviction that he is a servant of God, called to praise the Creator and to manifest the secret which unites spirit and nature. It need not be proved, because it is proved already by history, that art can never rise higher than the point where the artist takes his highest inspiration devoutly as a gift of the Creator. There alone art is safeguarded from false aestheticism and idolatry of genius, as well as from that formalism and barbarism which lead to the ruin of art.

The second direction which Christian faith gives to the higher culture is service of man. To be sure, science remains sound only where it is not dominated by the principle of utility. Art degenerates if it becomes subservient to any aim outside of itself. Purpose-free science and purpose-free art are identical with true science and true art. All the same, if this is taken as the last word, a perilous dualism results; somewhere there must be a unity between truth and beauty on the one side and the good life on the other. This connection, however, must be very high if it is not to degrade art and science. This highest unity is God. God is the origin of truth and beauty, as well as the Creator of nature and the body, and the source of the moral order. Apart from God there is no possibility of uniting the principle of service with the principle of disinterested search for truth and beauty. God alone, theonomy, is the guarantee that such disinterested quest, such "autonomy" of science and art, does not contradict ethical standards.

It is not at all necessary that art, in order to honour God, must be "religious" art or Church art; neither is it necessary that science should be subordinated to theology. Science and art serve men best if they remain true to their own laws. They must be "autonomous". But if this autonomy is ultimate, final, it cannot but degenerate into sterile inhuman intellectualist "scientism" and into *l'art pour l'art* aestheticism. If, however, their autonomy is understood as theonomy, they keep their independence and yet are united to natural life and ethical principles by a unity standing above all of them. This is not mere theory but historical experience. It is what we have learnt from the greatest men of science and of art. Filled with reverence for God, the ultimate source of truth and beauty, they remained true to the immanent law of truth and beauty. And in doing so, they served their fellow men much better than by any direct subordination to moral or utilitarian requirements. That is to say, the different spheres of higher culture have their autonomy, but at the same time they are linked with each other, not directly, not horizontally, but vertically, communicating with each other only by reference to the same source of their autonomy.

One last characteristic trait of the Christian idea of civilisation and culture relates to these two words as such. Why do we need two words, and which should take precedence? As everyone knows, there is a remarkable difference, again, between the German use of the words, on the one hand, and the English and French use on the other. In German it has become customary to think of *Zivilisation* as something much lower than *Kultur*, meaning primarily the technical aspect of what the English and French call civilisation. This degradation of "civilisation" is the result of that onesided idealistic spiritualisation which puts the purely spiritual things in the first place, calling them "higher" culture. The French and particularly the English use of words, however, is based on the high estimate of the civic element in all civilisation, the social and political element of justice and freedom, without which no true culture can exist. We need not repeat what has already been said in favour of this latter conception. It is a Christian heritage. Because in the Christian conception of man the relation between man and man is more important than the so-called "higher" culture, the problems of social and political order and, above all, those of marriage, family, and education, are basic in the Christian conception of civilisation and culture. We cannot put so-called higher culture in the first place, and therefore we cannot agree that civilisation be subordinated to culture. If we had to use one word only, we would rather use the word civilisation than the word culture, as we have done so far.

Having thus sketched the Christian idea of civilisation in rough outline, we can now, in conclusion, turn back to the very beginning of our lectures, to the question: What are the chances of a Christian civilisation in our age? The prospect seems to be very bad indeed, and we should not in closing make ourselves guilty of a false and facile optimism. Yet pessimism cannot be our attitude either. There is a German proverb: *Des Menschen Verlegenheiten sind Gottes Gelegenheiten.*[1] The terrible perspectives which are placed before us by the dechristianisation of the world during the past two centuries have opened the eyes of many of our contemporaries to the true foundations of civilisation and to the importance of the Christian tradition. It is not only the physicists and technicians, terrified by their latest results, that have become conscious of the imminent peril of human civilisation and are looking out for a new spiritual basis of life, but also the jurists, the sociologists,

[1] Man's extremity, God's opportunity.

the psychologists, and—last, not least—the artists and poets. The lowest point of secularisation seems to be behind us. In all spheres of civilised life there is a new search for the foundation of a really human civilisation, and in this search the Christian tradition is rediscovered. I do not prophesy an epoch of general return to Christianity, any more than I accept the myth of the Christian culture of the past. If I did, I should be guilty of a new kind of determinism, mistaking for predictable necessity what is a matter of decision. Mankind is confronted with a decision of incomparable consequence. All we can say is this: the decision *may* be made in the right sense, there is nothing impossible about it; but whether it *will* be taken in the right sense, nobody can know. It is sufficient that everyone who sees it should do what is required of him.

EPILOGUE

CHRISTIANITY BEYOND CIVILISATION

THE gospel of the redemption and salvation of the world in Jesus Christ is not meant to be a programme for any kind of civilisation or culture. Civilisation and culture, even at their best, are temporal; they belong to this earthly life. The gospel, however, is the revelation of eternal life. Civilisations and cultures come and go, just as man in his visible appearance comes and goes. But man as a person is not meant to pass away; he is destined by the Creator for eternity. That is why he is more than any culture or civilisation. The gospel of Jesus Christ is the revelation of this his destiny beyond and above historical life. To believe in this gospel means to be incorporated into the invisible world which is " beyond " and " above " the visible, that world the full manifestation of which will be the end of this visible historical world, with all its civilisations and cultures.

That is why the first and main concern of the Christian can never be civilisation and culture. His main concern is his relation to God in Jesus Christ, that life which is "hid with Christ ", his sharing in God's forgiving mercy in the fellowship with those who also, like himself, have become participants of God's revelation and redemption and of his firm hope in the fulfilment of God's promise of the eternal kingdom. This Christian faith therefore cuts across all forms of historical life with their different forms of civilisation, good and bad. It is not identical with any of them and none of them can ever be thought of as its adequate expression, All the differences between forms of civilised and cultural life are relative, whilst their distance from the eternal kingdom of God is absolute.

The Christian, then, and the fellowship of the Christians, are ultimately independent of all the changes—for good or evil—within the sphere of civilisation. They stand on a rock which no historical changes can move. Even the most terrifying anticipations for the further development of civilisation cannot—ultimately—shake, neither can any progress towards good confirm—ultimately—their faith in the final goal which God has set for all his universe and all mankind. The things of civilisation and culture, even their best, belong to "the flesh which cannot inherit immortal life". The Christian Church knows that no progress in the sphere of civilisation and culture can reach that goal of history beyond history, and that no setbacks, not even the complete destruction of civilised life, can deflect history from that ultimate goal which is beyond itself. In this sense then the Christian faith is indeed "other-worldly" and the Church should not be ashamed of saying so.

It is by this other-worldliness that true Christianity is "the salt of the earth" and "the light of the world". It is by its independence of the course of history that it can best serve the cause of a truly human civilisation and culture. It is by her very other-worldliness that the primitive Church of the first centuries gave the impulses for the best of those new forms of life which, with caution, may be called Christian civilisation. It is the paradox of the Christian existence that its other-worldliness proves to be the strongest force of renewal and preservation in the different domains of cultural life. Why this is so and how, we have tried to show in these lectures. God wants us to be in this world and to do our best in humanising and personalising its life. But we can render this service only when we know that this is not our primary but only our secondary task, as we keep ourselves free from all illusions of universal progress and of despair in sight of general degeneration and dissolution. Utopias are poor substitutes for real hope and despair is their almost necessary concomitant. In all times of Christian history it was those Christian men and groups of men who did not believe in progress who did the most to move the world in real progress. This creative and constructive contribution of Christianity to civilisation is, so to speak, a mere by-product of real Christian faith, but it is a necessary by-product by which its deeper reality can be gauged.

The problems of our present-day civilisation are so grave and pressing that even Christians may think it their duty to make them their primary concern and to consider belief in eternity as a kind of luxury. They are utterly wrong. The problems of our day have become so incomparably complicated and difficult just because people do not believe in eternal life any more. They are seized by a kind of time-panic. Not believing in the eternal Kingdom they try to make this world a paradise and by doing so they create a state of things which is more akin to hell than to heaven. The loss of real hope, i.e. hope in eternal life, creates utopias, and utopias may be considered as one of the main roots of our present-day chaos. If man loses the real hope he has to choose between illusions and despair, and mostly he vacillates between the two in a spiritual condition which the psychiatrists describe as " depressive-maniac ".

The real Christian is sober in his expectation for and from this temporal world. He knows that it cannot transcend its limits of death and sin. He knows also that it is the place where God can do marvellous things. He feels himself called upon by his Lord as His instrument by Whom he wants to do those things which man without the divine faith, love and hope cannot do. Still he knows that by all his doings the most he can achieve is to " salt " and to " leaven " the world, but not to save it from death and sin. And if he is a real Christian, he always is deeply conscious of his own shortcomings.

The Christian faith and hope in eternal life has been discredited, not without reason, during the last century, through having been used as a cheap substitute for justice and social responsibility. We cannot blame the Marxists for calling religion an " opium for the people " because that is what they all too often found it to be. There is, indeed, a false Christian other-worldliness which has done more harm to the cause of Christ than most other vices of Christian individuals and groups. But *abusus non tollit usum*. The false understanding of other-worldliness does not make the true other-worldliness false. Christianity which is no more other-worldly has ceased to be Christian. This other-worldliness is the root of true realism which hopes and works in and for this world without illusion and without despair.

God has created man for both this world and the world to come. He therefore made him capable of creating civilisation and culture and gave him the final destiny beyond them. It is the knowledge of this final destiny which makes Christianity capable of giving civilisation and culture an element which otherwise they do not have, the element of radical personalism and communalism, which are at bottom the same thing. A civilisation and a culture, as it would grow out of a truly Christian community, would be characterised by personalism and communalised creativity. But this very personalism and communalism is entirely the outcome of that faith and hope which have their roots as well as their aim beyond history.